BENCH TIPS FOR JEWELRY MAKING

BRADFORD M. SMITH

Bench Tips for Jewelry Making

101 Useful Tips from Brad Smith

Novel jewelry techniques, shortcuts, and suggestions to improve skills, save time, and increase quality of your work

First soft cover edition printed 2012

ISBN:0988285800

ISBN-13: 978-0988285804

DEDICATION

For whatever artistic abilities I have in jewelry and photography, I wish to give thanks to my Mom. For my underlying belief that a person can accomplish anything theyreally want to do, I am grateful to my Dad.

This project would not have been possible without the constant support, the unquestioned love, and the active collaboration from my wife and family.

The skills I've developed in jewelry are based on the expertise of my mentor, Anthony Chavez. I thank him for urging me to become a teacher and share the fun of making jewelry with others. It has become a rewarding and fulfilling part of my life.

I'd like to thank Robyn Hawk for her excellent seminars on social media. Her classes triggered my idea to start the BenchTips page on Facebook, which has led to this book.

Finally, I want to express my gratitude to my wonderful students for their generous support. I continue to learn more from them than they learn from me.

OTHER BOOKS BY THE AUTHOR

MORE BENCH TIPS FOR JEWELRY MAKING

ACCESSORIES FOR THE FOREDOM & DREMEL

MAKING DESIGN STAMPS FOR JEWELRY

BROOM CASTING FOR CREATIVE JEWELRY

THE RELUCTANT FARMER OF WHIMSEY HILL

https://amazon.com/author/bradfordsmith

CONTENTS

PREFACE

In every field, the top artisans have their favorite ways of solving common problems. Making a piece of fine jewelry is no exception. The work is intricate, but accomplished jewelers have a variety of alternative techniques, special tools, and shortcuts that save time and increase the quality of work. They're known as bench tips.

As a studio jeweler and a classroom instructor, I've always been interested in adding good bench tips to my knowledgebase. My students seem to find them helpful as well. As the tips grew in popularity and in number, I realized they might be of interest to other jewelers and decided to publish them in book form.

The material in these benchtips should be used only as a learning guide. Nothing in these tips is intended to negate the need for proper clothing, dust masks, and eye protection. All generally accepted industry safety procedures should be followed when using tools in the jewelry shop.

Happy hammering!

- Brad

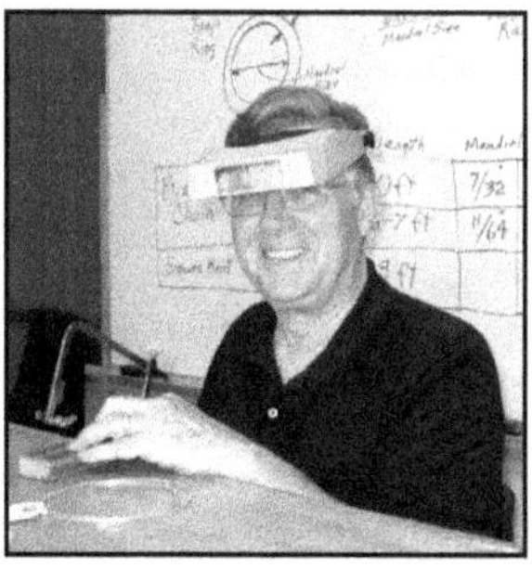

WARNING

Metal Working Tools and Procedures Are Dangerous

Do not attempt procedures described in this book without professional supervision.

All local and industry safety procedures should be followed.

CHAPTER 1

FABRICATION TIPS

BROKEN DRILLS

Have you ever broken a drill bit off in a hole? Sometimes you can grab it with pliers, but other times, the steel piece is below the surface in the hole. If this happens, a quick fix is to dissolve the steel in a solution of alum or fresh pickle. The solution will not affect a silver or gold piece.

Alum is typically available from a food store. Use about a tablespoon per cup of warm water. Submerge your piece so that the partially drilled hole is facing up to let the bubbles float free and not block the hole. After several hours, or overnight, any remaining drill bit should drop out.

CUTTING A BOLT

Whenever you have to cut a threaded bolt a little shorter, it is often difficult to get the nut to fit back onto it. And the smaller the bolt, the more difficult it is to restore the distorted threads. The problem is easily solved with the use of a nut.

First, screw a nut onto the bolt before starting to cut. Grip the bolt by the piece of the threaded end that will be sawed off. Then saw the bolt to the desired length, taper the end with a file or sandpaper, and unscrew the nut from the bolt.

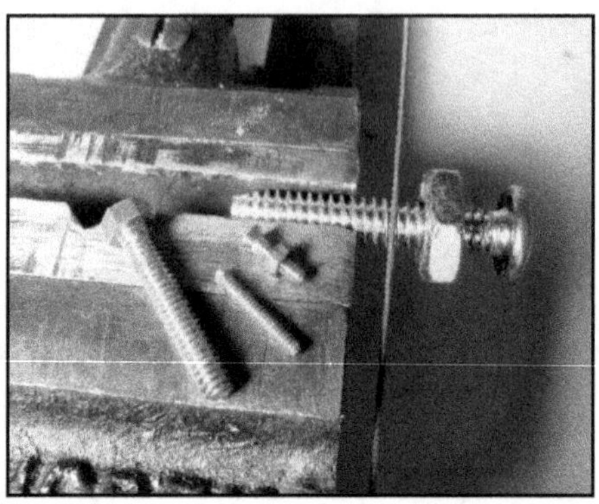

Unscrewing the nut over the freshly cut end of the bolt reforms any of the threads that may have become distorted and knocks off any burrs. Gripping the bolt by the piece to be sawed off localizes any crushing damage to the piece that you'll be throwing away.

DEBURRING A HOLE

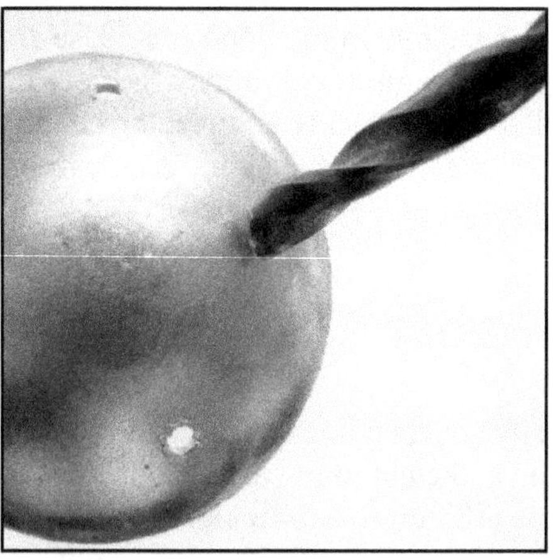

When drilling a hole, burrs are usually produced on the underside of the metal. Typically, burrs are removed by filing or sanding the area smooth, but doing it this way will put scratches on your piece that will have to be polished off.

A quick way to remove the burr is to grab a drill that's two or three times larger than your hole. Simply twist it in the hole to cut off the burr. I usually do this by twisting the drill in my fingers, but if you have many holes to do, it's easier on your fingers to put the drill into a holder like a pin vice.

DRILL BREAKAGE

Using a small drill is difficult for a beginner, especially if it is hand held in a flexshaft or Dremel. They are easily broken if pushed too hard or if tilted while in the hole. Many problems are the result of buying cheap drills. A good drill does a better job.

Remember that drilling always goes easier with lubrication. A little wax or oil is all you need. Almost anything will work – Three-In-One, beeswax, mineral oil, car oil, olive oil, or one of the commercial cutting waxes. The lubricant helps to move chips out of the hole and reduces friction of the drill against the side of the hole, keeping the drill cooler.

DRILL DEPTH GAUGE

Sometimes you need to drill a number of holes all to the same depth. One quick and easy way to do this is to wind some tape around the drill bit so that the tape just touches the part's surface when the hole is deep enough.

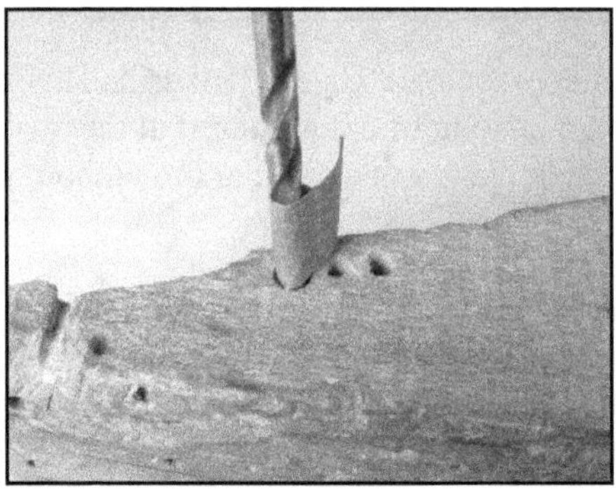

You can set the depth either by measuring from the tip of the drill to the tape or by drilling one hole correctly, leaving the bit in the hole, and wrapping tape around the bit at the surface level.

Note that a little extra tape left free on the end will blow away debris from the drilling.

DRILLING A STONE

One of the things my students often ask to do is drill a hole through a piece of gemstone. The usual thought is to get a diamond drill, but I've been disappointed with them. I think the reason is that the tip of the drill is just pivoting in the hole and fails to cut well. When the drill looks like it isn't cutting, the tendency is to push with more force. The drill gets hot, and the diamond grit falls off.

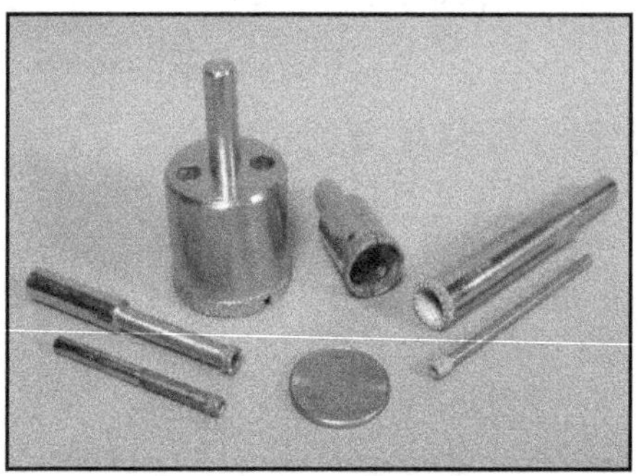

A more efficient approach is to use a core drill. This is a small hollow tube with a coating of diamond grit at the business end. The diamonds easily carve out a circular arc without undue pressure or heat buildup.

Core drills are readily available from lapidary and jewelry supply companies. They come in sizes as small as 1mm and are very reasonable in price. For instance, a 2mm diameter drill is about $6.

Chuck up the core drill in a drill press, Dremel or Foredom and be sure to keep the drilling zone wet to cool the tool and to flush out debris. Also, if you're drilling a through hole, go very easy on the pressure as the drill is about to cut through. Otherwise, you will usually chip off some of the stone surface around the hole as the drill breaks through.

FANCY RIVET HEADS

For a nice looking rivet head, use brass escutcheon pins. You'll have perfectly rounded heads that are all the same size and shape. The pins are a little hard to find, so try the best hardware stores first. Be sure to get solid brass pins, not brass plated steel. If unsure, test them with a magnet. Solid brass will not be attracted.

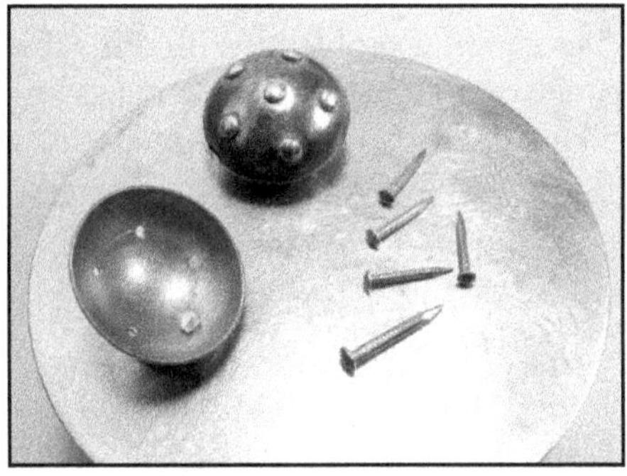

The pins are readily available online. Lee Valley Tools has them in 14 - 18 gauge and lengths from 1/4 inch up to 1 inch. Go to http://www.LeeValley.com and do a search for "brass escutcheon pin"

For best results, select a drill that gives you a hole with a close fit to the rivet Trim the rivet to a leave a little less than one diameter sticking out the back. Use a piece of hard plastic on top of your anvil or bench block to avoid flattening the head of the escutcheon pins while you peen over the back.

FIND THE BALANCE POINT

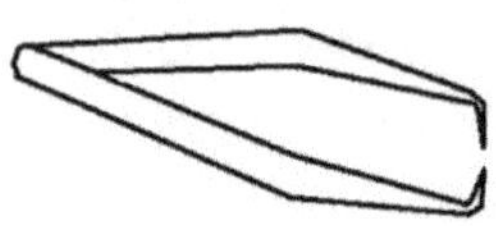

With odd-shaped pendants or earrings, it's often difficult to find the right place to attach a bail or loop so that the piece is balanced and hangs straight. A quick way to make a tool for this is to modify a set of tweezers. Any set of tweezers will work. Spread the tips, sharpen them with a file, and bend the tips at a right angle to point towards each other. To use the tool, suspend the pendant or earring between the two sharp points to see how it will hang.

GRIPPING SMALL DRILLS

Drilling small holes can be a problem. With drills that are less than 1 mm (18 gauge or .040 inches), some chucks will not tighten down well enough to hold the drill securely.

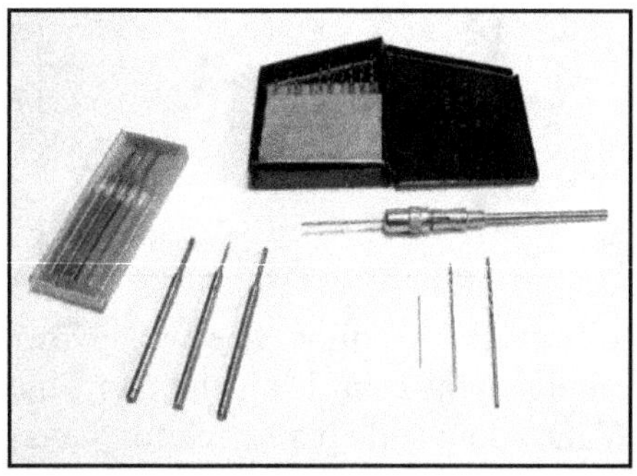

The problem is easily solved in either of two ways. The first is an inexpensive chuck adapter which has a 3/32 inch shaft. The other alternative is to buy the type of small drills with a 3/32 inch shank size. Either way gives you a large shank to be gripped by the drill press, Foredom, or Dremel, and changing bits is fast and easy. Both of these solutions are commonly available from most jewelry tools suppliers.

RING SIZE VARIATIONS

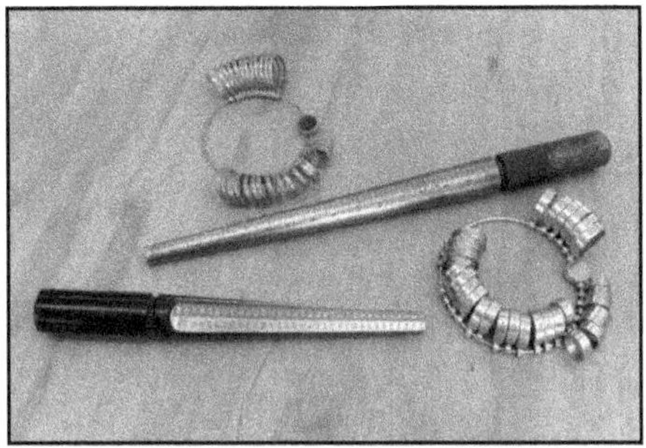

The numerical sizes marked on ring gauges and ring mandrels are often not the same across different manufacturers. If you're using a ring gauge to measure a customer, be sure to compare the markings on the gauge with the markings on the mandrel you use to make the ring. They may not be the same.

SETTING A RIVET

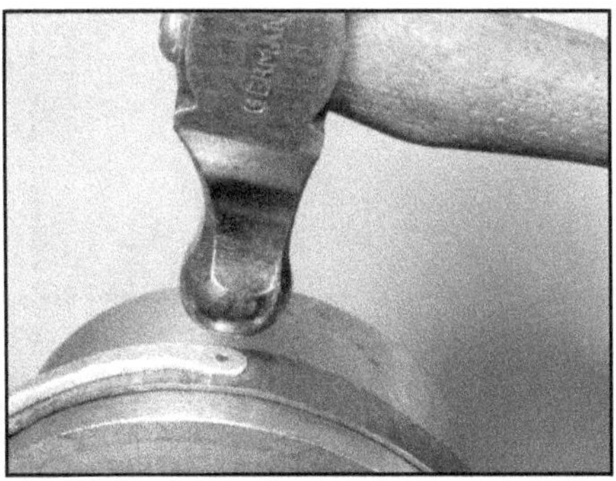

Riveting is usually done with a small cross-peen hammer, but I've found it's a lot easier for me to hit the rivet wire when using a small ball-peen. The smaller the better. I'm using one now that's about 3/8 inch diameter on the back of a chasing hammer, but I've been thinking that a 1/4 inch ball might be even better.

SAWING SMALL TUBING

When making a hinged bracelet, I needed to cut 16 pieces of small diameter silver tubing. These were to be just approximate lengths that would be trimmed to final size after soldering. Not having a tube cutter, I had trouble holding the tubing on the bench pin while trying to saw through it. The tubing was hard to keep from moving on the bench pin and tended to rotate as I sawed through it

Here's how I solved the problem. I drilled a hole in the side of the bench pin just large enough for the tubing to slide into and almost as deep as the length of cut tubing I wanted to cut. Sawing became quick and easy. With my free hand, I inserted the tubing and held it firmly from rotating while I sawed off each length.

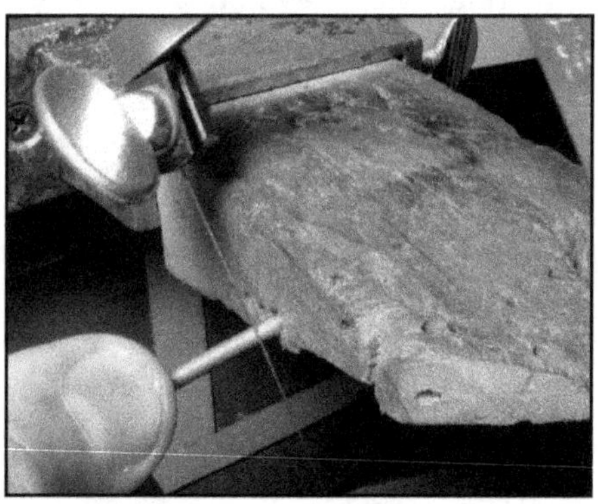

STRAIGHTENING WIRE

Have you ever pulled out some silver wire only to find it all bent up? The easiest way I've found to straighten it out is to stretch it a bit. Simply put one end in the vise and grab the other end with a pair of serrated tip pliers. Then pull just enough to feel the wire stretch like a rubber band. This works best on smaller wire diameters, up to about 16 gauge.

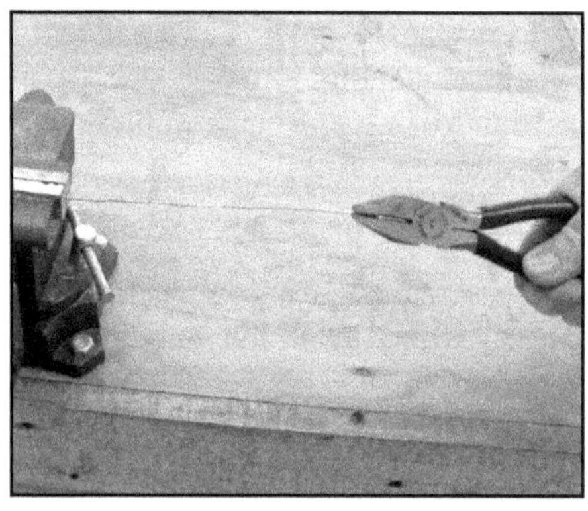

Be careful if you are trying to pull hard on a thick wire. Be sure to brace yourself in case the wire breaks or pulls out of the pliers.

TAPERED REAMERS

A tool you don't see often these days is a tapered reamer.

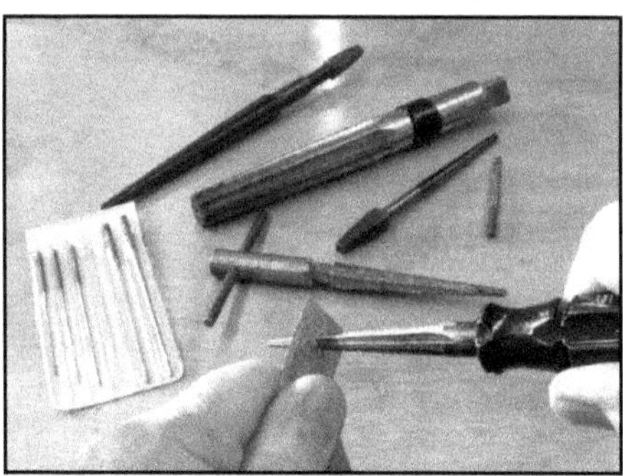

They're particularly useful for making an irregular hole round or for enlarging a hole to an exact diameter. For example, the small set in the yellow pouch is for holes in the range of 0.3mm to 2.5mm. They are great for sizing a tube to fit a hinge pin. Other times when I'm drilling a hole for riveting and can't find the exact size drill, I simply drill the holes with a slightly smaller bit and enlarge them with a reamer until the wire just fits.

For larger hole sizes in sheet metal up to 14 gauge, I really like the reamer with the black handle. It makes quick work of sizing holes from about 3mm to 12mm. You can find them in well-equipped hardware stores.

You may never use the larger diameter reamers shown in the background, but after sawing out some rings from 4mm thick bar stock, I found they worked well for rounding out the holes.

TWISTING WIRE

Twisting wire can be done with a hand drill but goes much faster with a power tool. My preference is to use a screw gun, although a Foredom should do well.

Just make a little hook out of coat hanger wire (or use a screw-in cup hook) and chuck it up in your screw gun. Fasten the ends of the wires in a vise and slip the looped end onto your hook. Keep a little tension on the wires as you twist.

Note that a power drill is too fast for this unless you have one with a variable speed control.

USING YOUR THUMB

When using multiple bits in your Foredom, you often have to deal with several different shaft sizes - the usual 3/32 inch burs, the larger 1/8 inch shaft sizes, and of course the many different sizes of twist drills. For some reason I really dislike having to turn the key multiple times to open or close the jaws of the handpiece chuck.

There are two ways to speed up that task. For opening up the jaws, I just remember "four", the number of turns I have to make to open the chuck just enough to insert the larger shaft.

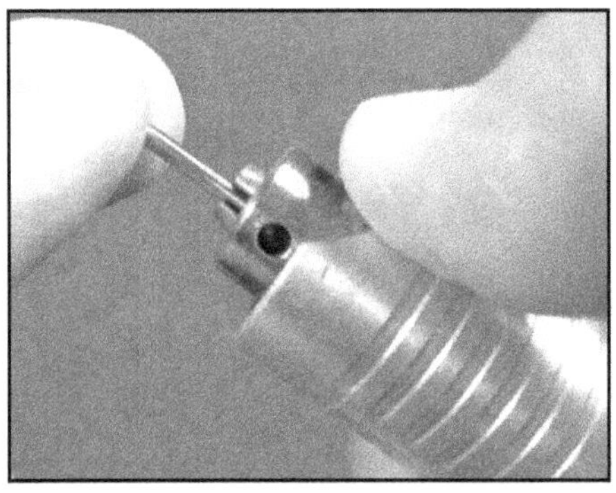

For closing the jaws around a smaller shaft, there's a neat trick. Hold the new bit in the center of the open jaws of the chuck, put your thumb lightly onto the outer toothed collar of the chuck, and gently start up the Foredom. As the chuck turns, it will naturally tighten the jaws around the shaft or the drill bit. Then just tighten with the key.

CHAPTER 2

FINISHING TIPS

CLEANING STEEL SHOT

Steel shot in a vibratory or rotary tumbler works great to burnish and shine your finished silver pieces. But a common problem is how to keep the shot clean. Carbon steel shot can get rusty if exposed to the air, and even stainless steel shot can sometimes develop a blackish coating that is hard to remove.

My solution of choice to clean the shot is Classic Coke. Just pour an ounce or two over the shot and let the tumbler run for an hour or so. A bad case might require a second cleaning. Some folks like to let the bubbles in the Coke dissipate before using it so that gas pressure doesn't build up in the tumbler barrel. I've heard that it's the phosphoric acid in Coke that does the trick.

While you're waiting for the shot to clean up, just settle back and enjoy the rest of the Coke.

EMERY BOARDS

Sanding boards for doing your nails are one of my favorite finishing tools. I like the ones with a thin foam core. They have enough resistance to sand just the high points off a flat surface but give a little when you're trying to smooth a curved surface.

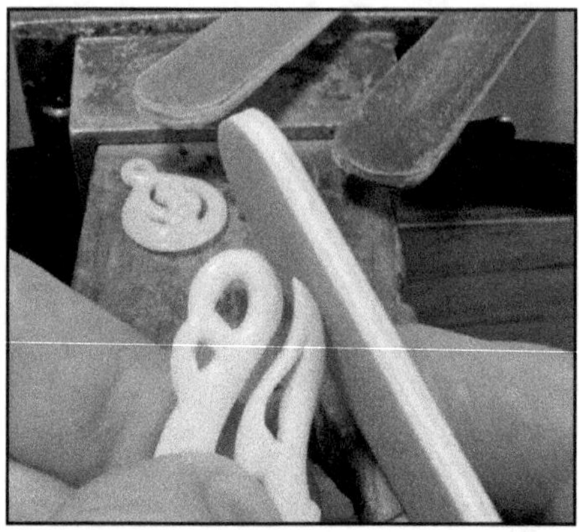

Plus they're inexpensive and come in a variety of grits. Some grits are so fine they give an almost finished surface. Pick up a few at a beauty supply company or at your local drug store.

FINISHING CUTOUTS

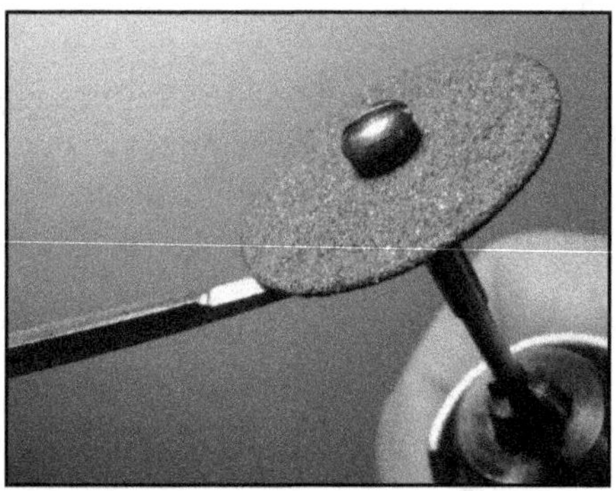

After sawing patterns there's always a little cleanup to do, and the smaller cutouts can be a challenge. Needle files (7-8 inches, 190mm) can get into the larger cutout areas, and Escapement files (4 inches, 100mm) can get into some of the corners. But I often find myself looking for even smaller files. I couldn't even find them at a watchmaker tools supply company, so I had to try something else.

I ended up grinding down the tip of a 4 inch barrette file using a separating disk (or cutoff wheel) in the flexshaft. Be sure to wear your safety glasses when using this tool. A flake of steel in your eye makes for a bad day.

PATINA RECIPIES

In a recent class, we did a little work with patinas. I came across a couple web sites for those of you who'd like to explore this area, especially for copper and bronze.

The first is The Science Company at http://www.sciencecompany.com/Do-It-Yourself-Patina-Formulas-W12C672.aspx with plenty of formulas for a variety of colors. And there are more formulas at Tim McCreight's Brynmorgen Press web site at http://www.brynmorgen.com/resources.html

Small quantities of chemicals for making your own patinas are available from The Science Company at http://www.sciencecompany.com/Patina-Chemicals-C672.aspx

If you prefer to buy the patinas already for use, one of the best sources I've come across is a company called Sculpt Nouveau at http://www.sculptnouveau.com/

Don't miss all the instructional pdf's on their site, and be sure to take a look at the videos showing how to use their products at http://www.youtube.com/sculptnouveau

POLISHING WHEELS

In the finishing sequence, there's a step called pre-polishing between sanding and buffing. One of the most effective tools I've found to help here is the little silicone wheels used in a Foredom or Dremel. They come in several different abrasive levels and several different shapes. The wheels are color-coded to denote their abrasive level.

Different shapes (coin, knife, cylinder, point, etc) are available to match the geometry of the area being cleaned up.

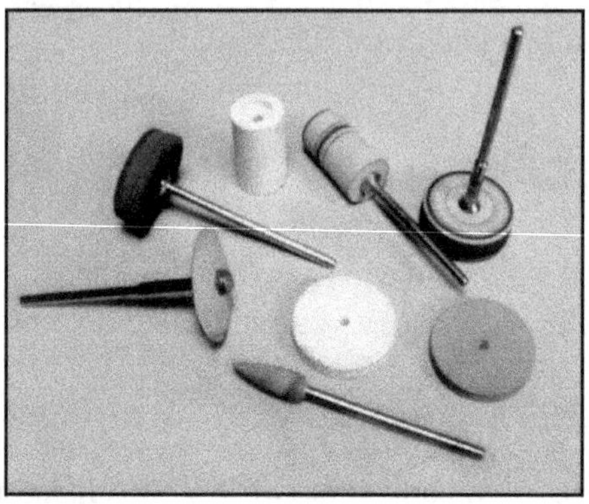

For a starter, I'd suggest a medium, a fine and an extra fine wheel in both the coin shape and the knife-edge shape. The thicker coin shapes are particularly handy. Be sure to get a few extra mandrels so you'll have one of each wheel shape mounted and ready to go.

Cylinder shapes are nice for doing the inside of rings. Knife-edge shapes clean up the base of bezels quickly. Most jewelry catalogs carry these wheels, but often the color codes don't match between different manufacturers.

PROTECTING SURFACES

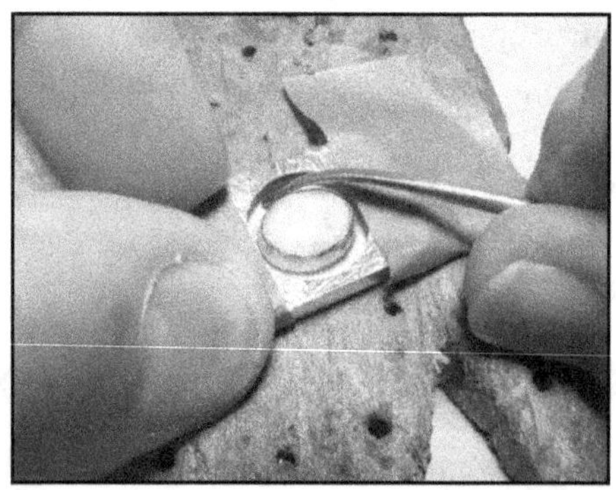

I figure that any accidental scratch I make on a piece means about 15 minutes of extra sanding and polishing. So after finishing major surfaces I typically cover them with some masking tape to avoid any scratches when doing final work like cleanups and setting of stones. The blue masking tape used by painters works particularly well because it doesn't leave a sticky residue.

TOUCHING UP A BEZEL

Pumice wheels in your Dremel or Foredom are good for touching up a bezel after you've set the stone. The hardness is about 6 on the Moh's scale, less hard than quartz, so it shouldn't scratch citrine, amethyst, or any of your jaspers. However, I'd avoid or be very careful of using pumice near the softer stones like turquoise, amber, Howelite, etc.

If you're unsure that a wheel is pumice, test it with a piece of glass. Glass is about the same hardness. If it doesn't scratch glass, it shouldn't scratch quartz.

My preference is the one inch diameter ones such as those shown at riogrande.com/Product/AdvantEdge-Pumice-Wheels-Medium/332722?pos=2

RESHAPING WHEELS

Silicone polishing wheels in the Dremel or Foredom are a great time saver, but after using them a bit they often need to be reshaped. This is particularly true with the knife-edge wheels.

The natural thought is to grab one of your files and hold it up against the rotating wheel to reshape it. But this causes a problem. The grinding grit in the silicone wheel is much harder than the steel in your file. This means that you will end up grinding down the teeth of your file.

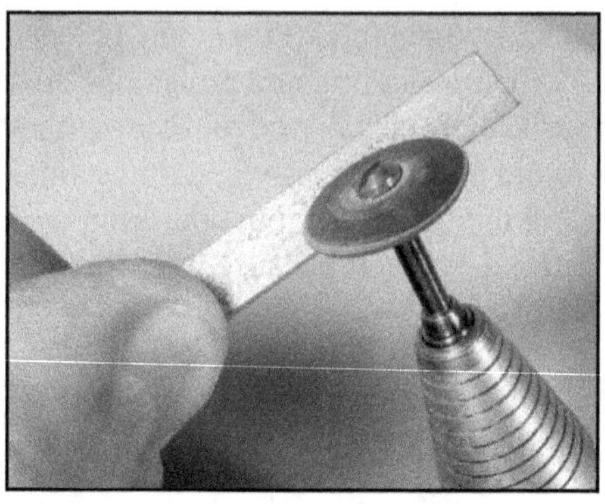

The best way to reshape your polishing wheels is to use a diamond file. If you don't have one and must use a steel file, I choose to sacrifice the area of the file that is closest to the handle. That's an area which is not used in normal bench work.

SANDING DISKS

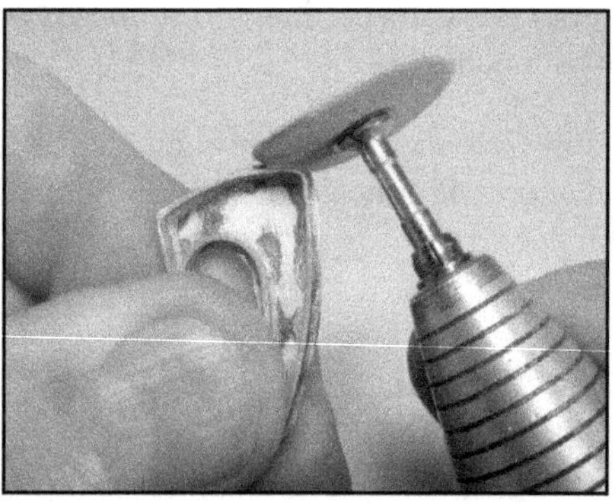

One of the flexshaft tools that saves a lot of time is the snap-on sanding disk. I mainly use the medium and fine grits but sometimes like the very fine ones sold for working with platinum.

Ordinarily, you'd think of placing the disk on the mandrel with the grit side facing away from your hand, but notice that you end up with your elbow up in the air. Instead, I flip the disk so that the grit side is towards my hand. It's a much more comfortable position. The elbow is down near my side, letting me hold the work up close where I have a better view of what I'm sanding.

I use these snap-on disks so frequently that I keep multiple mandrels with different grits already mounted in the bur stand. Some mandrels have the grit facing out, and some have with the grit facing in.

SANDING TIGHT SPOTS

Often you'll need to sand or polish an area that's hard to reach with even a small wheel on a flexshaft. Other times it might be the bottom of a pocket or inside bottom corner of a box that needs to be finished. One trick for these nit-picky jobs may be left over from your last Chinese dinner - a chopstick.

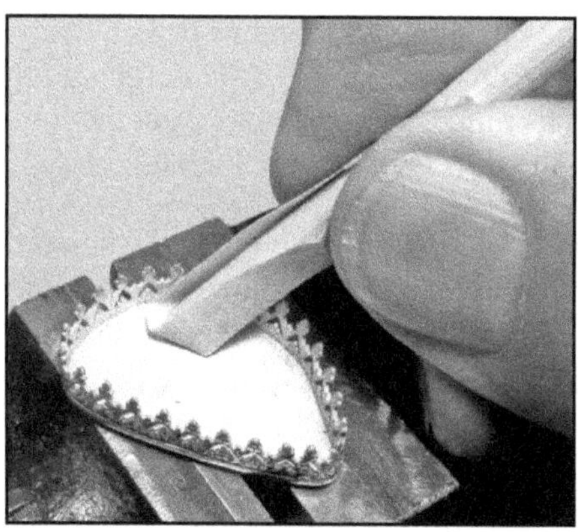

I've found quite a few uses for these in the shop. Prepare the tip by sawing it off at a 45 degree angle. For abrasive, you can use either a strip on sandpaper held over the tip or some loose abrasive grit, Tripoli or rouge. If you don't have any loose grit, you can always scrape some off a piece of sandpaper. Mixing the grit with a bit of petroleum jelly or oil to help keep it on the end of the chopstick.

SMOOTHING EARWIRES

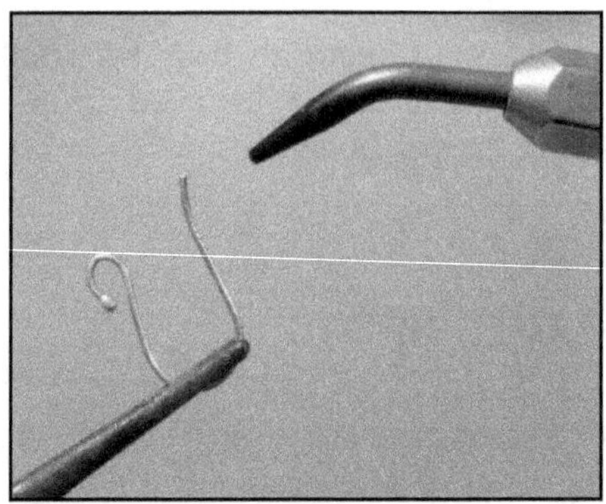

Any time you make your own earwires, the hardest part for me is to sand and polish the end that's inserted into the ear. Any sharp edge there is no fun. I've tried using sanding sticks, cup burs, and silicone polishing wheels. I've tried buffing on a Zam wheel. I've tried spinning the wire in the Foredom to polish the tip. While these techniques all eventually get the job done, none are very easy, and none are as fast as I'd like.

Then it occurred to me - I could melt the wire smooth. One quick touch in the flame of the propane/oxygen Little Torch does the trick - not enough to form a bead on the wire but just enough to round off the tip. I find it's worth practicing the maneuver a couple times on some scrap wire before trying it on completed earrings.

SPOT SANDING BRUSH

Sometimes you have some discoloration or debris to clean from the bottom of a pocket, from an area of coarse textured surface, or from a small space between two soldered objects. Finding something to get into those close areas is always an effort in creativity.

One tool I have for these special occasions is a glass fiber spot sanding brush. It's great for cleaning a small area and doesn't leave deep scratches - only a faint satin finish.

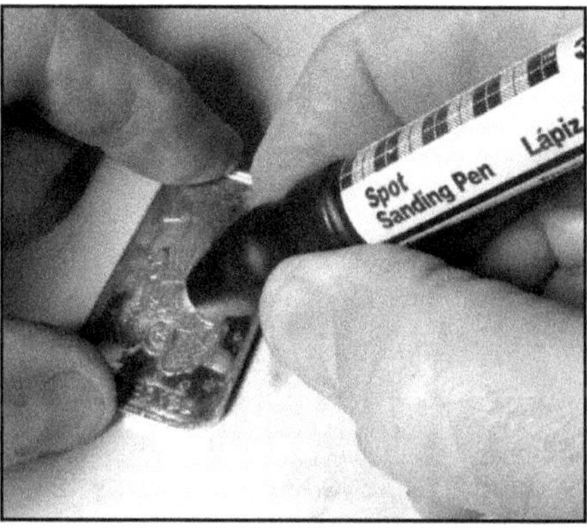

There are probably several manufacturers of these pens, but one is the PrepPen Adjustable Sanding Pen. You can see it at http://www.amazon.com/Prep-Pen-PrepPen-Adjustable-Sanding/dp/B000J18RT6/

STIFFENING EARPOSTS

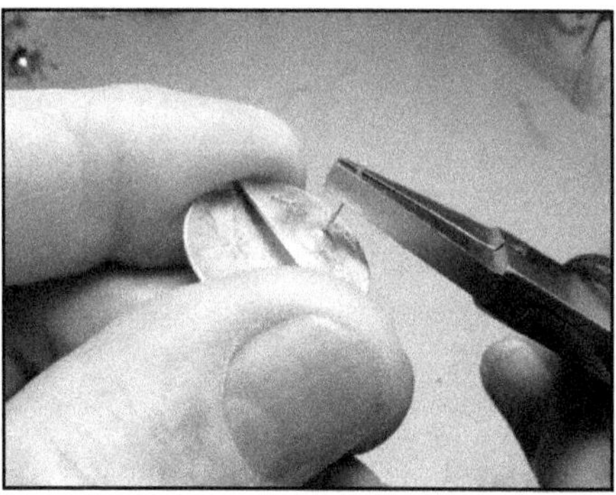

Soldering an earring post will always soften the wire a bit. The easiest way I've found to harden it is to grip it with pliers and twist it a couple half turns. This work hardens the wire and also tests your soldered joint.

REMOVING A STONE

If you've forgotten to use dental floss and got your stone caught in a bezel, there's one thing you can try before starting to pry. Find some sticky wax or beeswax. Roll it into a pencil-sized cylinder and stick the end onto the top of the stone. Mold it on well and yank.

But if the stone is really stuck or if you need to remove a stone that had already been bezel set, there are two solutions. But each has risks and consequences. The first is to pry the bezel open with a small, sharp knife blade. Be very careful not to wrinkle or tear the bezel while doing this. Work all the way around the bezel prying it open just a little bit the first time. Pry it open a little more on a second pass, and keep enlarging the bezel until the stone is loose enough to drop out.

The other way to remove a stone is to drill a small hole into the bezel setting from the back side so that you can push the stone out. This does leave a hole, but if the stone has a polished bottom, you can convert it into a design feature by sawing an interesting design out of the metal.

CHAPTER 3

CHAIN MAILLE TIPS

MANDRELS

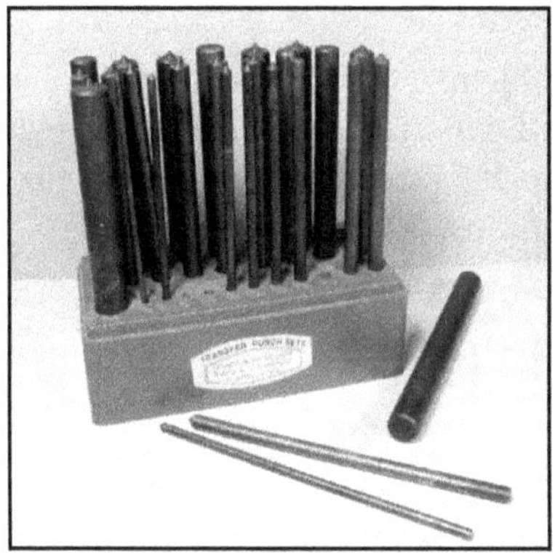

Straight rod mandrels have a multitude of uses in helping to bend sheet and wire. Frequently, we choose a round rod for winding jump rings. Common sources for different sized rods are knitting needles, wooden dowels and clothes hangers. Metal rods can also be found in hardware stores and hobby shops.

But to get the right "look" in chain maille designs, you must have just the right size mandrel, and often they are not easy to find. Jewelry catalogs sell selections of straight rod mandrels for $50 or more, but my choice is from Harbor Freight. They have a set of 28 sizes, from 3/32 inch to 1/2 inch.

It's called a Transfer Punch Set. The catalog number is #3577, and the price is about $12. Plus, look for the 20% off coupon on any one item in their advertising circular. That cuts your cost even further. I've bought four of these over the last couple years. www.harborfreight.com

DEBURRING JUMP RINGS

When cutting jump rings from large gauge wire for chain making, you'll notice the saw leaves a small burr. An easy way to remove these is to tumble the rings with some fine-cut pyramids. It's best not tumble for a long period with the pyramids because it will remove the polished finish from the wire.

No tumbler, no problem. You don't actually need a tumbler. I just put a handful of pyramids in a wide mouth plastic jar and shake for a bit. You can find these pyramids in the tumble finishing section of most jewelry supply catalogs.

MODIFYING PLIERS

Sometimes a few changes to your tools can make work go faster and improve the quality at the same time. Stock tools can be customized and improved using standard jewelry skills. Here's an example:

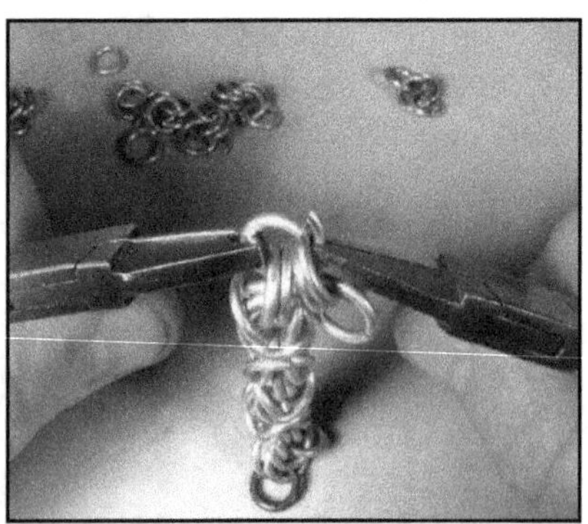

While making a lot of chain maille, I noticed I was ending up with a few scratched jump rings that required extra cleanup time before the chain could be polished. So I started looking into what I was doing wrong.

Making jump rings and weaving them into chain maille designs involves a lot of opening and closing of the rings. I typically use two square jaw pliers to do this, one for each hand. The jaws of my pliers were pretty much scratch free. On a new tool, I typically relieve any sharp edges, sand away any tool marks on working surfaces, and give those areas a quick polish.

That helped but was not the whole problem. While making chain, the rings would sometimes slip out of the pliers or slide within the jaws as I was trying to twist them closed. I noticed the jaws close at an angle, and that gave me the idea of forming a groove at the end of the jaw that would help grasp a jump ring without scratching it. Not only have these pliers worked well for chain maille, but I've found several other problem jobs that this modification solves very nicely.

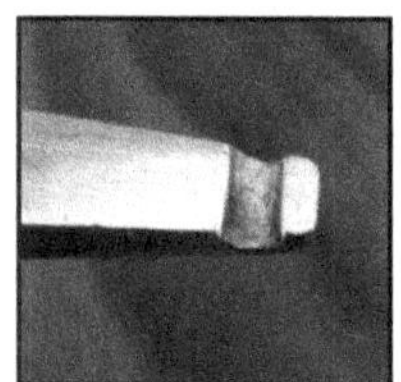

To make up what I needed, I bought two inexpensive sets of square jaw pliers. My preference is for jaws that are about 3.5 - 4mm wide. This provides a good fit for the jump rings I use. It's important to have enough metal at the tip of the jaws to accommodate a groove that's deep enough. If the tips are too thin, just cut them back a bit. Locate and mark the position on the jaw where the thickness is about 1.5mm.

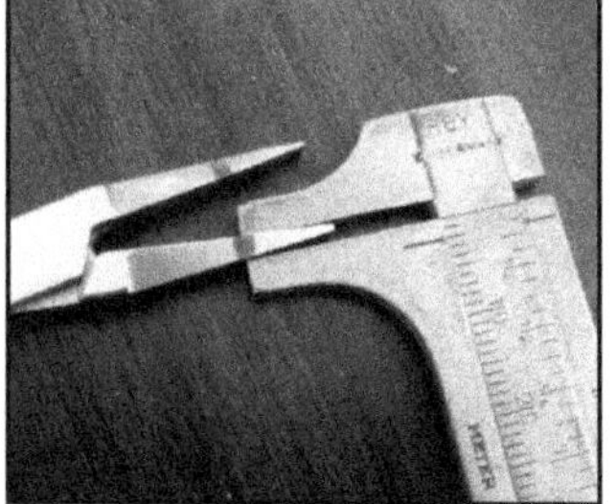

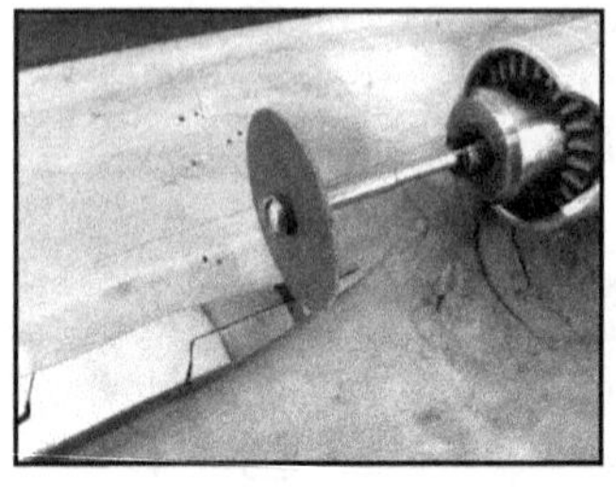

Cut the tips off with a separating disc or grind them off with a bench grinder. Remember when cutting or grinding metal, good safety glasses are a must. Also, if you use the cutoff wheel, be sure to hold and brace both the workpiece and the handpiece securely. If either moves, the disk will break.

Start forming the grooves by making a cut with the separating disc in one jaw. Close the pliers and mark both ends of the groove on the opposite jaw. Then cut that groove with the separating disc.

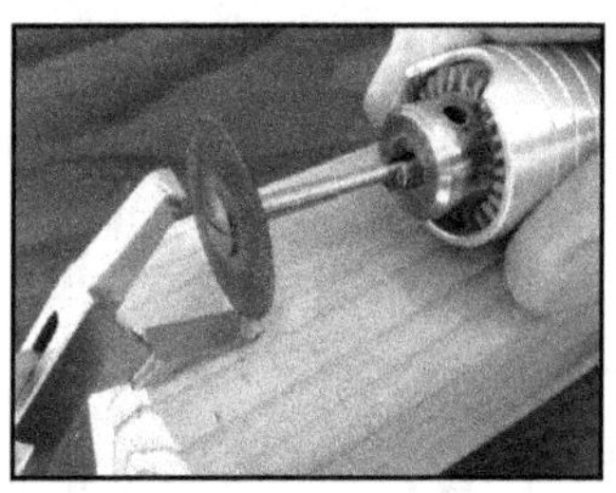

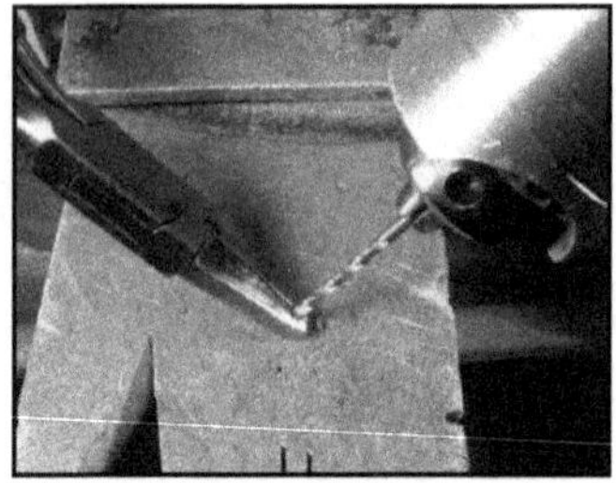

Now to make the grooves round so they grasp the wire without distorting it, I close the jaws and run a drill through the opening formed by the two rough grooves. I start with a small drill and follow up with a drill just slightly smaller than the wire size I want to grip. Here it is 14 gauge wire, so I chose a #53 drill.

Next, the shape of the grooves needs to be refined. I used a coarse, knife-edge, silicone polishing wheel on the flexshaft to polish off all marks left by the drill and to round off the outer edges of the groove.

Finally, test for proper fit by laying a jump ring into each groove. In particular, look at the way the edges of the groove contact the inside of the ring. The groove may need to be widened at this point to avoid having the pliers leaving a nick.

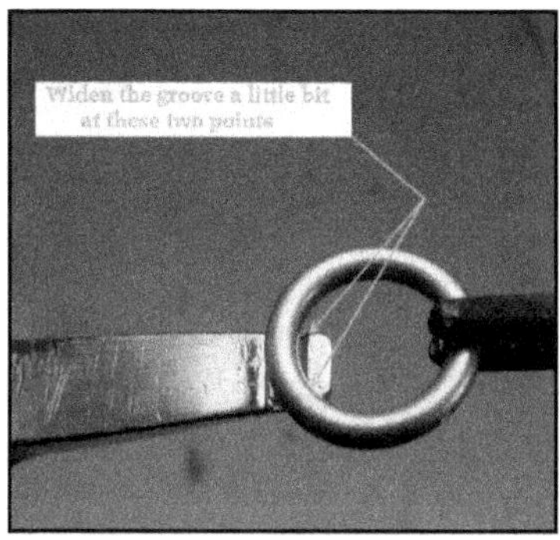

Do a final polish on the jaws so they will not leave any scratches as they grip a ring. I used a medium grit, knife-edge, silicone polishing wheel to get into the groove.

SAWING JUMP RINGS

The difficult part of making jump rings for me has always been holding the coil while cutting off the individual rings. I use a saw to get the best fit when closing the rings later.

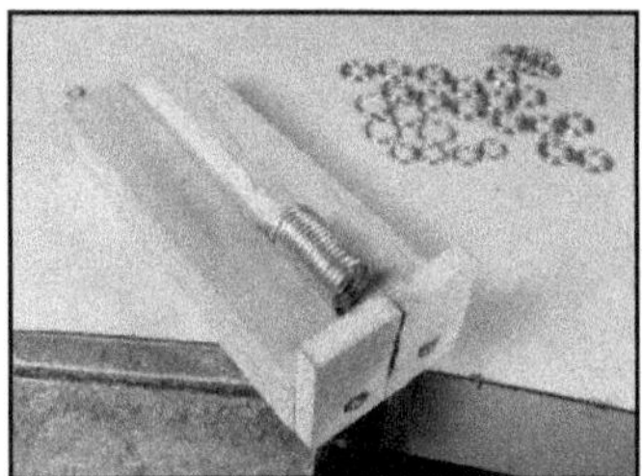

I've seen all sorts of suggestions for ways to hold the coil of wire, but the one that works best for me is this little jig made from scrap wood. It's about 2 inches wide and 4-5 inches long with a groove cut down its length to cradle the coil of wire and a thin stop attached to the front end.

To cut the rings, thread the saw blade through the coil, hold the coil down in the groove and against the front stop. Then saw through the bottom of the coil at about a 40 degree angle.

Don't forget to use some cutting lube or wax. It really makes a difference. Check how well it works with a simple experiment. Count how many rings can be cut before the blade breaks.

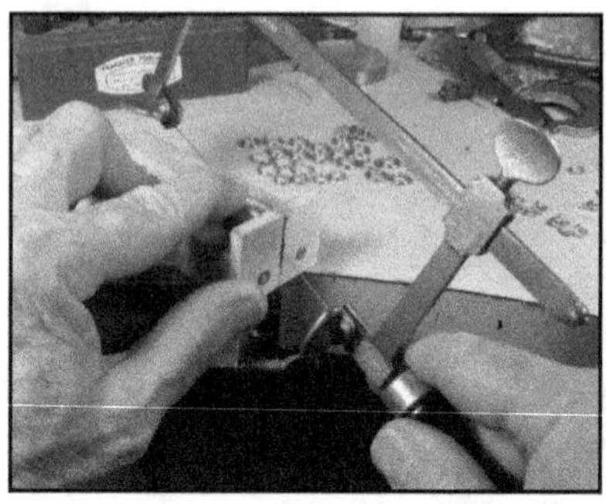

Do the test first without lube. Then do it again adding some lube to the blade after cutting every 8-10 rings.

WINDING JUMP RINGS

Winding a few jump rings around a rod is easy. But when you need a lot of them, some form of winder saves a lot of time. A variable speed screw gun makes quick work of it. Screw guns are quite inexpensive at discount stores and are remarkably handy for odd jobs in the shop and around the house.

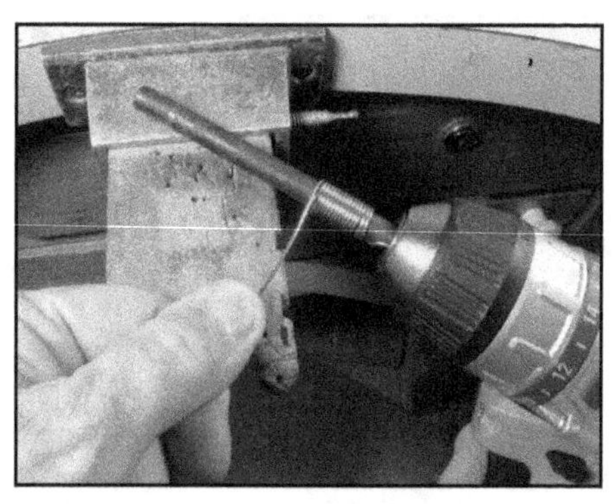

To wind a coil just bend a right angle on the end of the wire about a half inch long and insert this into the screw gun chuck. Wind slowly, keeping a tight coil. Often I rest the end of the mandrel on a table or on the side of the bench pin.

Finally, one note of caution. When winding an entire length of wire, be careful to stop winding before the end of the wire passes under your thumb. It can cause a nasty scratch.

CHAPTER 4

MATERIALS TIPS

DENTAL GOLD

One might think that a couple pieces of dental gold would be valuable. But if there is only a small amount, it can actually be a problem. Sending it to a refiner is expensive for small amounts of metal.

I made the mistake of thinking I could melt it and roll out my own sheet. However, the trace metals that dental gold contains to make it a good material in your mouth cause it to crack if you try to forge it or roll it out as a sheet. It ruined my whole ingot.

So what to do with a couple gold crowns? If you have enough material to do a casting, that's probably the best use for dental gold.

If you're not into casting, try melting it on a solder pad and while molten, divide it into small pieces with your solder pick. Then re-flow each piece to make little gold balls for use for accents on your designs. The balls can also be planished a bit to make small discs or struck with a design stamp to add texture.

USE A SPRAY BOTTLE

A good way to store firescale preventers and debubbling solutions is in one of the little spray bottles you can find at the drug store.

SOLVENT DISPENSER

Frequently, I need to fill a small bottle with alcohol, like the bottle of an alcohol lamp or a nail polish bottle that I use for the yellow ochre anti-flux. Often I can't find a small funnel and end up spilling almost as much as I get into the bottle. It's wasteful, and the fumes aren't too good for you either.

A neat and inexpensive solution is to use a lab dispensing bottle to store small quantities of the solvents most frequently used. The bottles have a wide mouth for filling and a fine tip for dispensing. You can get a small stream or just a drop or two. With the bottle's fine tip I don't spill a drop.

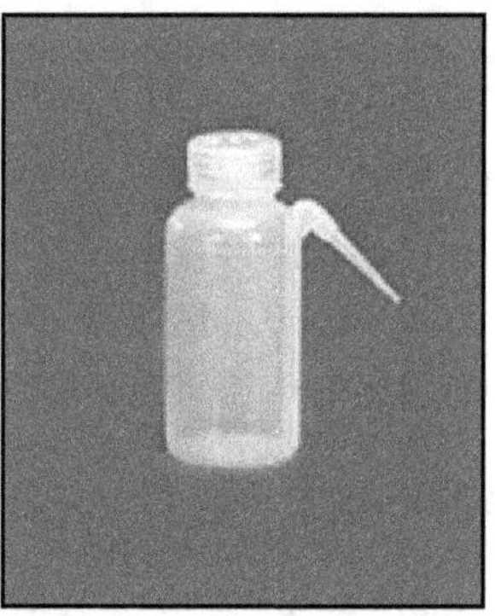

A Google search will turn up many suppliers. One I've used is Carolina Biological Supply Company at www.carolina.com The bottle is Catalog # 716580 Unitary Wash Bottle, Low-Density Polyethylene, 125 mL. They have several sizes including some labeled for specific solvents.

LOCAL METALS SOURCE

Local sheet metal shops typically have barrels of scrap copper, brass, and aluminum sheet that they save for recycling. The shop owner will usually let you go through it to select the shapes and thicknesses you want. Prices vary but will generally be just a little more than the wholesale per-pound scrap value.

I've found it's much cheaper to buy metal this way than ordering from a catalog. There are no shipping charges, and you'll be supporting a local small business. Just remember to bring your thickness gauge and work gloves.

SECRET INGREDIENT

Those of us who use paste solders sometimes find an old tube has dried out. There should be some way to recondition it, but what to use? Calling tech support at the suppliers didn't work. Either they don't know what to use or won't tell you the secret.

None of us likes to waste an expensive material, especially at $16 - 20 a tube, so I've often experimented with ways to rejuvenate it. Mixing in a liquid flux doesn't work. When the liquid starts to boil off, it spatters the solder in all directions.

But after several failed experiments, I finally found a way that does work. My secret ingredient is petroleum jelly. Mix in just enough to restore the consistency to something that's usable.

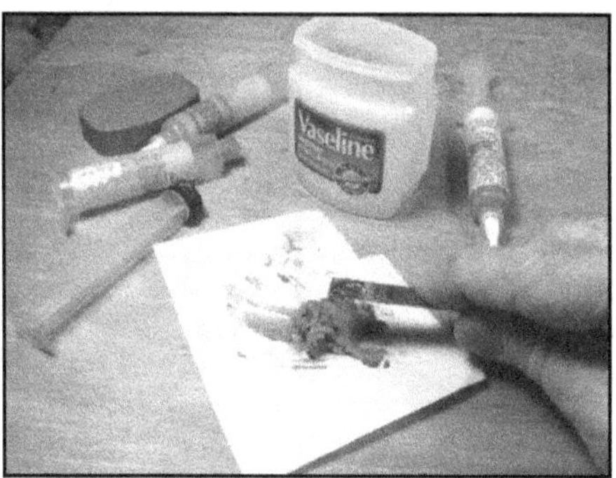

If your solder is in a syringe, it can be a little difficult to get the plunger out. I find the easiest way is to poke a hole through the solder from the tip to the rubber plunger (a bur shaft was the right size for my tube). That lets in the air so you can slowly withdraw the plunger. Once the solder is out of the tube, you can easily add the petroleum jelly, mix it up, and spoon it back into the syringe.

SOURCE FOR PLASTIC

We often use plastic in our studios, like for a single part die or for a template. So it's handy to have a small supply along with the rest of your sheet, wire, copper and bronze. But we seldom think to buy and stock any plastic.

The plastics store I go to has a scrap bin out back where they give away small pieces and scraps. I usually just go for the 3/8 and 1/2 inch thicknesses for use as forming dies, but there's always a variety of sizes and colors to choose from including thin sheets that are good for templates.

If you can't find a shop with Google or Yellow Pages, do a search on Ebay.com for scrap plastic by the pound.

JUST A DROP

Hobby shops and model airplane stores carry small plastic dispenser bottles that are handy bench items for applying a drop of oil or glue just where you want to put it. The length of small metal tubing coming out the top lets you squeeze out very small drops.

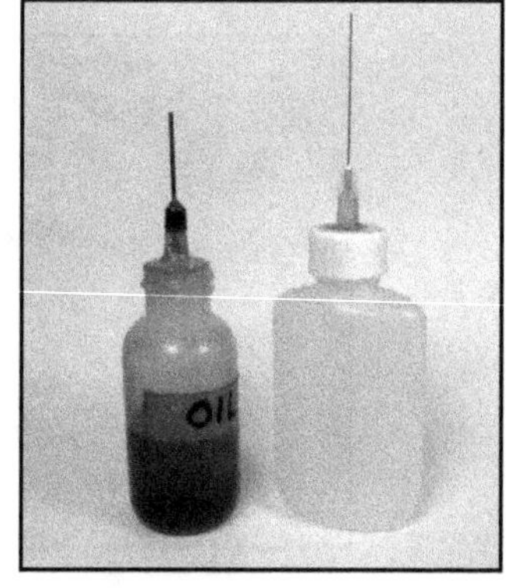

I use one with a short length of tubing for oil when I'm sawing or when drilling harder metals like steel. Another bottle I found in a plastics store has a longer length of metal tubing on it used for dispensing fast drying glues to join pieces of acrylic. The long metal tube let's you reach into tight places. Either of these is handy for flux at the soldering station.

LITTLE BALLS

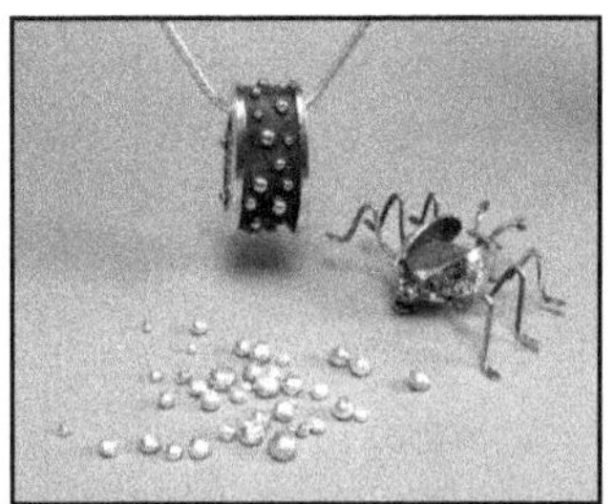

Little balls of silver and gold make nice accent pieces on many designs. They can be made as needed from pieces of scrap. Cut the scrap into little pieces, put them on a solder pad, and melt them with a torch. Then throw the balls into a small cup of pickle.

If you need to make all the balls the same size, you need the same amount of metal to melt each time. The best way to do that is to clip equal lengths of wire. But there's an easier way to get a good supply of silver balls. Some casting grain comes in near perfect ball form. Just grab some tweezers and pick out the ones you need.

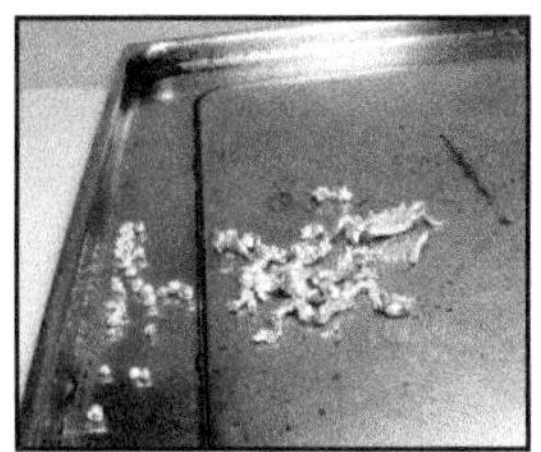

For larger quantities of balls, pour the casting grain out onto a baking pan, tilt the pan a bit, and let all the round pieces roll to the bottom. Bag the good ones and pour the rest back into the casting bag. Balls can be sorted into different sizes using multiple screens.

TESTING FOR SILVER

Often you need to identify some of those unknown "silvery" metal pieces in the bottom of the toolbox or some piece of old jewelry. Is it silver or something else?

Of course, if you need to know exactly what you have, it's best to send your metals off for refining. But inexpensive silver testing solutions can be used to help distinguish higher silver content alloys from alloys that have the same appearance but with little to no silver content, like German Silver or Nickel.

I purchased a half-ounce bottle of JSP Silver Testing Solution #GT41. It's not a rigorous analytic test, but it tells you if you're on the right track. And it's inexpensive. Mine was only $3.

With a fresh solution you have an instant reaction after applying it to the metal being tested. The procedure is simple - as you apply a small drop, look for a color change. Note that the acid will leave a slight mark, so choose a spot that is out of the way or will be easy to polish.

If you suspect the object is silver plated, you should file a little notch somewhere inconspicuous to expose what metal is below the surface. Otherwise, all you test will be the surface plating.

Here's the reaction I got when testing various materials:

Fine Silver	Red/Orange
Sterling Silver	Brick Red
80% Silver 20% Copper	Dark red changing to gray
Brass	Yellow changing to blue
Nickel	Gray-green
Copper	Yellow changing to blue
Steel	Black
Stainless Steel	No color change

Caution - If you do any of this testing, know that you are handling a reasonably strong acid. The GT41 label says it includes nitric acid and potassium dichromate.

Wear safety glasses.
Don't get any testing solution on your skin.
Wash and clean up well when you're done.
Always have a solution of baking soda and water handy to neutralize acid.

WAX WITH ADHESIVE

Often I want to increase the thickness of a model by adding a layer of wax on the back side. For instance, thin models like a leaf or a flower petal do not cast well unless you add extra thickness. The problem is trying to apply a coating of wax that's smooth and even.

I found a new product that solves this problem. It's an easily moldable sheet of wax with an adhesive coating on one side. This lets me easily add thickness to a very thin model. For instance, press it onto a leaf, trim the wax to the leaf shape, and then gently bend the resulting sandwich to the contour you want. The wax is available in a number of different thicknesses starting from 26 gauge all the way up to 14 gauge.

If interested, the supplier is:

> Jewelry Tools & Supplies
> 412 W. 6th Street #1011
> Los Angeles, CA90014
> 213 624-8224
> jtstech@sbcglobal.net

CHAPTER 5

SHOP ORGANIZATION TIPS

SHEET & WIRE STORAGE

The more you work with jewelry, the more problems you have finding the piece of metal you need. My pieces of sheet were generally stored in various plastic bags, and the wire was in separate coils. Few were marked, so it often took me a while to locate that piece of 26 gauge fine sheet I bought last year especially since I usually take my supplies back and forth to classes.

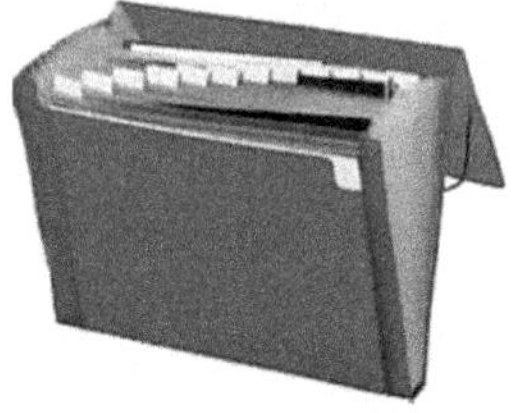

A tip from a friend helped me organize everything. I bought an expanding file folder from the office supplies store (the kind that has slots inside and a folding cover). I marked the tabs for each gauge of metal I use. Then I marked all my pieces of sheet with their gauge, put them in plastic bags, marked the gauge on the bag, and popped them into the folder. I usually store coils of wire loose in the folder, but they can also be bagged if you prefer. I use one tab for bezel wire and one for miscellaneous items.

The resulting folder is really convenient when I want to take my metal out to a class or workshop. It's also colorful enough for me to easily find it in the clutter of the shop!

MAGNETIC TOOL BAR

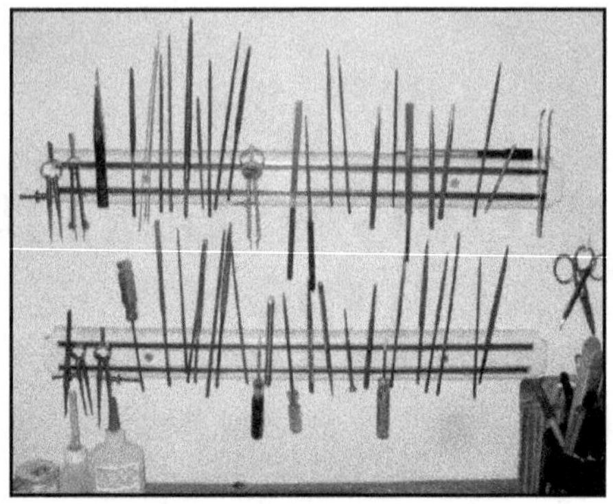

An easy way to keep all your files organized at the bench is to use a magnetic tool strip. They're not expensive and help keep a lot of small tools from cluttering the bench top. I got a couple of them from Harbor Freight for about $5 each. Go to http://www.harborfreight.com and search for “magnetic holder”

MANAGING PRODUCTION

Many jewelers sell their jewelry at shows, in galleries or online. They are sole proprietors constantly under pressure to design new pieces while making enough product to keep up with demand. So their options are few when a large order comes in. They can burn the midnight oil themselves, or they can be smart and get some temporary help. But you need good help, and you often need it fast.

Jewelry assemblers are skilled, trustworthy, and reliable craftsmen who make it their business to help others handle overloads and meet deadlines. Flexible arrangements are possible, working by the job, by the hour, or by the piece. Each has a different mix of skills, from fabrication to enameling, casting, stone setting, lapidary, and others.

Assemblers are known to the trade, so you may have to ask around to find some references. But some assemblers advertise on the Net. For instance, a good friend of mine, Janice Metz <JenFT4@aol.com>, has been working with designers and fabricators in the West Los Angeles area since 1997. She specializes in silversmithing, wire-wrapping, and beading.

MOBILE FLEXSHAFT STAND

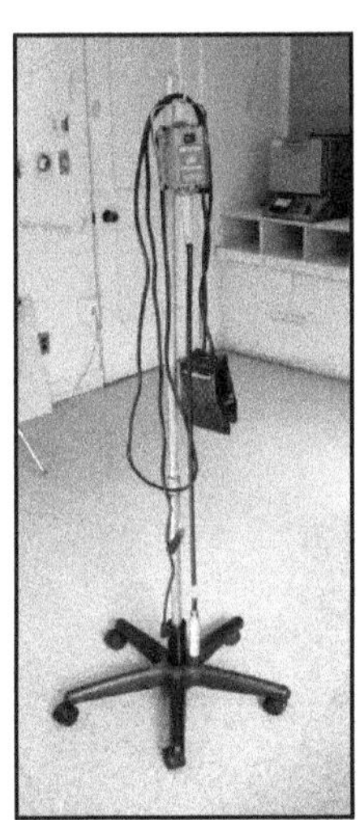

A handy mobile stand for the flexshaft can be made easily and quickly from the base of an old swivel office chair. Chairs are thrown out frequently at office buildings and schools. When I needed one, I just asked the custodian in my building to set one aside for me.

The stand is made from two pieces of threaded galvanized steel pipe and a pipe fitting from the hardware store or a plumbing shop. The first length of pipe is 3/4 inch diameter to fit the hole in most chair bases. The second piece is a length of less expensive 1/2 inch pipe.

The total length of the two pipes should be five feet. I used a two foot length of 3/4 pipe and a three foot length of 1/2 pipe. They are joined together by a pipe fitting called a 3/4 to 1/2 reducing coupler.

To separate the chair from the wheeled base, simply remove the spring clip from the center bottom. I use a small screwdriver or a pair of pliers.

STORING SMALL PARTS

With all the little components we use for our projects, it makes sense to have a good way to keep them organized and prevent them from getting lost. A great small container to use is available for free at your local drugstore. Ask at the photo processing area for some of the 35mm plastic film cans. They have a tight fitting lid and are great for carrying beads, findings, jump rings, and silver scraps.

With the popularity of digital cameras and smart phones, the 35mm film cans are getting a little scarce, but my photo processor still saves them for me.

CHAPTER 6

SOLDERING TIPS

AVOIDING SOLDER LINES

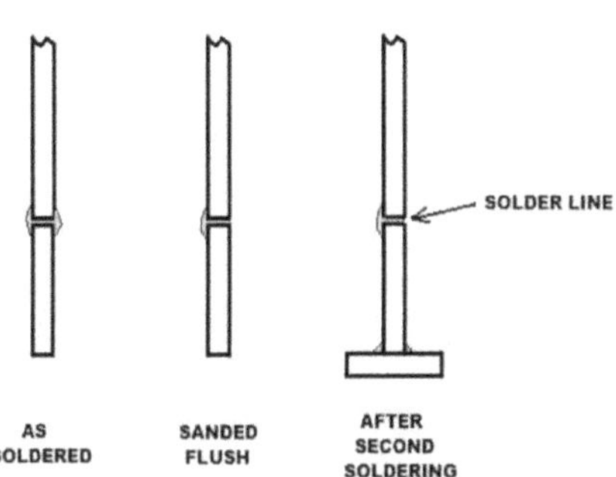

After finishing a soldered joint on say a bezel, have you ever seen it reappear after you've soldered the bezel to a base plate? What's happening is that every time a piece is heated to soldering temperature, the liquid solder seeps a little more into the surrounding metal. This leaves a small furrow where the solder had been sanded off flush at the joint. To get rid of the furrow, you have to re-sand the joint area down to the bottom of the furrow.

To avoid this when I have another soldering operation to follow, I try to leave a little extra solder on my joints. For instance when trimming off excess base plate from around a bezel, I leave a paper thickness of excess plate material whenever possible until I'm done with all soldering.

Of course, this isn't always possible as when a soldering operation will prevent you from gaining access to an area for final sanding and polishing.

CHEAPER & BETTER PICKLE

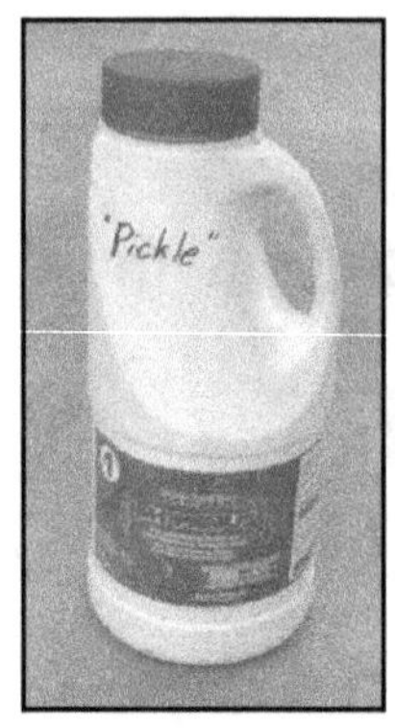

Most jewelers use a granular pickle mixed with water. The active ingredient is sodium bisulfate. This can be purchased from local stores as a common pool chemical used for adjusting the acidity of the water. It's sold under various names, so be sure to check the list of active ingredients for a brand that is 95% or so sodium bisulfate.

An added benefit is that the pool chemical is more pure in form than what is sold for jewelry use and does not cause the brown grime often found floating on the top of the pickle pot.

IDENTIFYING SOLDERS

Despite the many ways to mark your sheet or wire solders, I have sometimes forgotten to do it and had a couple that I could not identify. The answer is to compare the melting temperature of the unknown with that of a couple known solders.

What I do is take a thick scrap of copper or nickel and arrange several solders on it. Ideally, I would have a sample of easy, medium, and hard known solders surrounding the unknown solder. Then I heat the plate from the bottom and watch the order in which the solders melt.

OCHRE APPLICATOR

Yellow ochre is used when you want to be sure the solder won't flow on an area of your piece while you're soldering another area. The only problem with ochre is coming up with a good way to store and apply it.

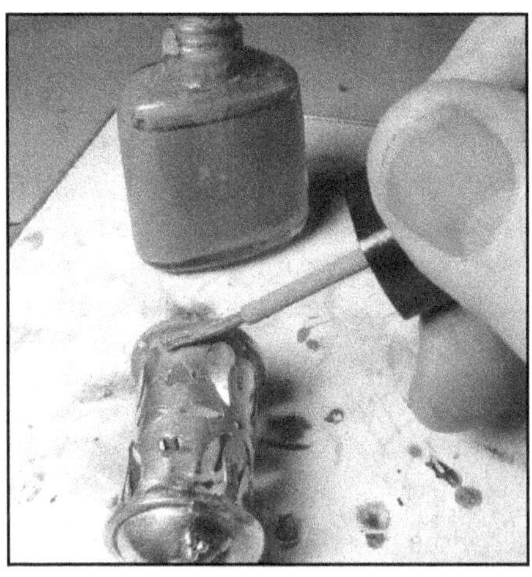

I use recycled nail polish bottles. They seal well and have a built-in brush applicator. Just clean them out with a little acetone or nail polish remover, and they're ready to go.

SILVER DISCOLORATION

Working with jewelry involves an ever increasing number of skills. Chemistry is one of them that comes into play when dealing with a discoloration on the metal caused by a chemical reaction between it and the environment.

In the case of Sterling silver there are three discolorations we typically encounter: a tarnish, a firescale, and a firestain. Each is different in its cause, in its cure, and in its prevention. All three have to do with the metals in the Sterling alloy (92.5% silver and 7.5% copper) and how they react with oxygen and the heat of soldering or with pollutants in the air over the long term.

Tarnish is a grayish coating that builds up slowly on the surface as a result of a reaction of the silver with sulfur-based compounds in the air. Typically these are pollutants from the burning of petroleum fuels, but they can come from other sources as well. I once tarnished all the silver in my display case by putting a pretty specimen of iron pyrite in with the jewelry. Turns out pyrite has sulfur in it!

Sulfur from air pollution or any other source combines with the silver to form a grayish silver sulfide film on the surface. Preventing tarnish involves keeping sulfur away from the metal. Plastic bags will help, and anti-tarnish strips are available from jewelry supply companies to pack near your items. Tarnish is easily removed by hand polishing with a jeweler's cloth or with one of the products sold for cleaning the good silverware for holiday dinner.

Another way is to remove it chemically. Put a piece of aluminum in the bottom of a dish large enough to contain your piece. Heat enough water to cover the silver. Mix in 2 tablespoons of sodium carbonate per cup of water and pour into the dish. Be sure the silver touches the aluminum. Sodium carbonate is the main ingredient in washing soda. Read the labels in grocery and hardware stores.

The second type of tarnish is called firescale. It is the dark gray to charcoal colored film that forms on Sterling or other copper alloys like brass or bronze when we heat it with a torch. The copper in the alloy reacts with oxygen in the air to form a dark cupric oxide coating on the surface. Luckily, the oxide is easily removed by dissolving it in a mild acid - generally called a pickle. It's important that we not let firescale form on a solder joint because it will block the flow solder over the joint.

There are two ways to prevent firescale. Most common is to use a flux, a borax-based solution applied to the metal before soldering. When melted, borax forms a thin glassy layer that keeps oxygen away from the metal. A second way is to do your soldering on a charcoal block. Together with the flame, charcoal greatly reduces the amount of oxygen in the area being soldered. In either case, oxygen is prevented from reaching the metal, so no cupric oxide firescale is formed.

A second oxide can also be formed when soldering copper or a high copper content alloy like bronze or brass. It's called cuprous oxide and is reddish in color. That's why a black looking piece you put in the pickle sometimes comes out red. The problem is that while the black cupric oxide is dissolved by a pickle, the red cuprous oxide is not. The discoloration can be sanded or polished off, but an easier way is to use a "super pickle". This is a mixture of fresh pickle with a healthy shot of hydrogen peroxide from the local store.

I've saved the worst form of discoloration -firestain - for last. Think of firescale (above) as like getting dirt on your shirt that you have to wash off. Firestain is like getting ink on it. The discoloration is not just on the surface, it seeps down and stains the material. Firestain happens when we heat a piece of silver too hot, too long, and/or too many times.

Firestain occurs when the oxides start to build up below the surface of the metal. You generally don't notice it until after polishing. It appears as a darker area of the surface and is easy to spot when viewed under light bounced off a piece of white paper. Because firestain is below the surface, there is no easy bench tip solution. Depletion gilding may work for some pieces. Otherwise, removing it calls for sandpaper and aggressive polishing.

A much better approach for a piece that will require a large number of solderings is to protect the metal from developing firestain by applying liberal amounts of a firecoat. Regular soldering flux will provide some protection but is not as effective as preparations made specifically for the task.

Jewelry supply companies offer several commercial solutions, but my favorite is the Prips mixture. I use it every time I intend to do more than two solderings on a piece.

SOLDER FROM SCRAP

Sometimes you need a lot of silver solder to complete a piece the way you want it to be. For me, it was when I was trying to join several castings. Silver solder is expensive. So I found a way to make my own from scrap with a little help from a penny.

The first step is finding out what's in a solder. A search through the reference books (Tim McCreight or Erhard Brepohl) or a Google search will turn up recipes like:

Hard - AG 80% CU 13% ZN 7%

Medium - AG 70% CU 20% ZN 10%

Easy - AG 63% CU 30% ZN 7%

The silver (AG) and the copper (CU) are easy to come by, but finding some zinc (ZN) has always been my problem until I found out that our pennies are almost all zinc. According to Wikipedia a U.S. penny minted after 1982 weighs 2.5 grams and is 97.5% ZN and 2.5% CU. So all I had to do is add a penny to some copper and a pile of silver scrap.

Since I was using Sterling scrap, I had to adjust for the amount of copper in it as well as the amount of copper from the penny. Here's what I used for components of medium solder:

Sterling - 36.90 grams

Copper - 9.35

Penny - 2.50

Melt the silver and copper first in a melting dish, mix well with a carbon rod or titanium solder pick, add the zinc (penny) last, mix again, and pour into a small mold. The zinc is added last because melting it causes some to vaporize, and the fumes are a safety problem (they're a nasty gray-green color). Be sure to have good ventilation.

To check the solder's melting temperature was correct (medium), I put a sample of the homemade solder on a piece of copper sheet along with a known sample of hard, medium, and easy solders. I then heated the plate from the bottom and watched as the easy first melted, the medium melted, the homemade melted, and finally the hard.

Additional notes on converting the ingot to sheet, strip, or wire form - If you have access to a rolling mill, that will be the fastest way to proceed. Either roll out the ingot into a sheet and cut strips, or roll it out as wire if your mill has the grooves. If you don't have a mill, all you have to do is forge out the ingot into a rough sheet of the gauge you'd like and then cut thin strips with bench shears. Be sure to anneal the sheet every so often as you forge it.

SOLDERING EARPOSTS

I don't solder enough earposts to develop the dexterity for holding the wire by hand. So I modified a set of locking tweezers to help with the job. It's quick and easy.

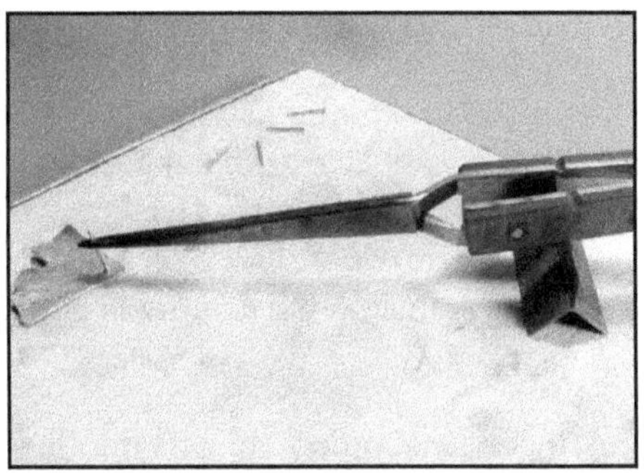

Use a triangular file to make a notch at the tweezer tip to keep the wire from moving around. File a groove in the tweezer body to rest the tweezers on a stand that keeps the ear post wire at the right angle. The stand is just soldered up from scrap copper or nickel.

This way the tweezers act like a see-saw that's weighted just a little bit more on the soldering end. I felt that if the tweezers put too much pressure on the ear post wire, it could buckle when the wire gets up to soldering temperature.

SOLDERING PRONGS

I often use prongs to hold an irregular cab or other object on rings and pendants. But prongs are a little tricky to solder. You have to find some way to hold them all upright while soldering. The simple butt joint that looks strong sometimes breaks when you start to bend the prong over the stone. There's nothing worse than having a prong break off when you're setting the stone.

I solved both problems with one little trick. It keeps the prongs in position for soldering, and it gives you a stronger joint at the same time. Locate and centerpunch the position for each prong. Then drill holes a little smaller than your prong wire. Sand a small taper on the ends of your prong wires, and stand them up in the holes. The wires support themselves. Soldering is easy. The joint is stronger because of the increased soldering area.

SUPER PICKLE

We've all made the mistake of putting some steel in the pickle, causing all your pieces to be coated with copper. Easiest way I've found to clean it off is to fill half a coffee cup with new hot pickle and put in an ounce or two of hydrogen peroxide from the drug store. Put your pieces in, and the coating is gone in about 10 minutes.

Many people think that when some steel gets into the pickle, the solution is contaminated and should be thrown away. Not true as long as you can remove all the steel from the pickle. In fact, the pickle should work even better after the steel is removed.

Pickle works by dissolving the copper oxides that form on the surface of copper bearing alloys exposed to the heat of soldering. Pickle gets "old" when it cannot hold any more dissolved copper. Putting steel in the pot forces some of the copper to come out of solution. This allows more copper oxides to be dissolved.

LASER WELDING

Jewelers often encounter very delicate soldering operations. For instance how to solder closed several jump rings that hold blue topaz briolettes onto a necklace. We have all heard about ways to do some soldering close to a stone, and some of us have sized rings without taking the stones out of their mounts. We've used wet paper towels, garnet sand, cooling gels, or we have suspended the stone in a dish of water. All techniques bank on the principal of using a small, hot flame to do the job quickly before the stone gets hot and cracks or changes color.

Each job is somewhat of a gamble. Some stones are hardy, and some are frail. Jades and jaspers will generally take some heat, while others like topaz or opal are easily damaged. Trying to shield a stone from the torch is always a betting game, and sometimes you lose.

If soldering something close to a stone is too risky, perhaps it's time to consider a no-heat method like laser welding. Most jewelry stores have laser welders these days, and the cost of having it done is quite affordable. They used to have problems doing silver, but now seem to do it routinely.

I've used a local shop twice in the last year, once for a piece with little emeralds a friend asked me to repair and a second time for a silver bracelet where I needed a safety catch and didn't want the torch heat to expose all the solder lines again. The jeweler solved both problems perfectly.

CHAPTER 7

STONE SETTING TIPS

BEZEL PROBLEMS

When bezel setting a cab that has rather sharp corners, have you ever had problems pushing the metal down at the corners? It's a common problem often causing a wrinkles or folds in the bezel.

In order for a bezel to capture the stone, the top edge of the bezel must be compressed and become shorter to lay down onto the stone. With a round or oval stone, compression naturally happens as you push and burnish the bezel. But when setting a stone with corners, the tendency is to push the long sides of the bezel down first. No compression happens along the sides. A, and all excess metal is left at the corners. Compressing everything there is difficult. Often the only way to remove the extra metal at the corner is to make a saw cut and fold the two sides in to touch each other.

If you want a smooth bezel all around the corners, the simple solution is to set the corners of the bezel first. Then push in and burnish the sides. In this way the necessary compression is distributed along the length of all sides and not forced to occur at the corners.

With the corners set first, the top edge of the bezel can easily be compressed along the sides.

BURNISHING BEZELS

A dapping ball can sometimes be used to burnish a bezel. I noticed this when setting some 10 mm cabs on a piece of filigree. It was difficult to get enough pressure with a regular burnisher, so I tried a dapping ball and found it much easier.

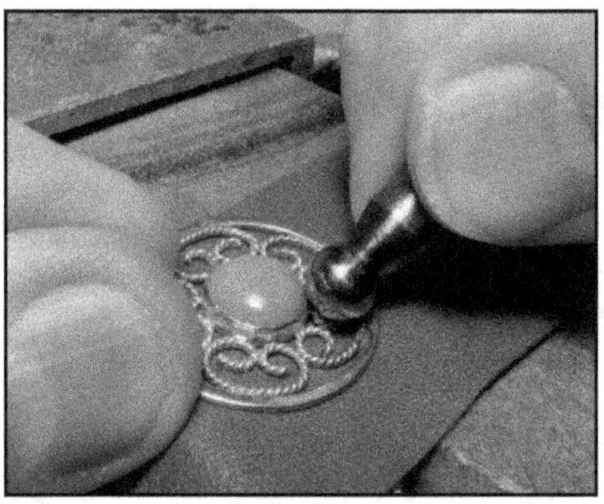

Make sure the ball is well polished (hit it with the Zam wheel), and let it ride along the base of your piece. Select a ball big enough so its curvature hits the top of the bezel at the best angle to burnish it down onto the stone.

DENTAL FLOSS

When testing the fit of a stone in the bezel, it's all too easy to get it stuck. If tapping the finding or opening up the bezel a bit with a knife blade doesn't dislodge it, you might have to drill a small hole in the bottom and push it out with a needle.

To avoid all this frustration, lay a piece of dental floss over the top of the bezel before you seat the stone. Then just pull on the string to remove the stone.

EASIER PRONG SETTING

When setting stones in a prong mount, the tool is less likely to slip off the prong if you grind a groove into its face or rough up the face a bit with sandpaper. Some folks prefer a prong pusher for doing this, and others like a set of pliers.

The easiest way to create a slot on the pusher is with a file, and the easiest way to create a slot on one jaw of your pliers is with a cutoff wheel. Then do a rough polish on the slot with a medium grit, knife-edge silicone wheel.

PRE-MADE BEZEL CUPS

As a general rule of thumb I assume it's going to take me 15 - 20 minutes to make a bezel for an ordinary cabochon. For some projects, buying pre-made cups can save a lot of time. If you go this route, keep in mind three things. First, try to get cups made from fine silver, not Sterling. Fine silver is softer and burnishes over the stone more easily.

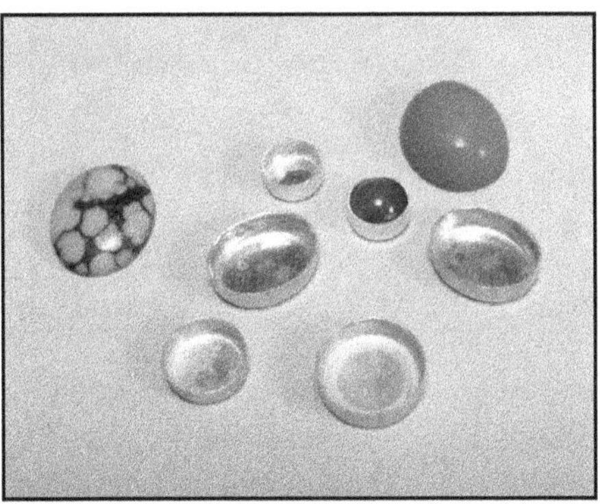

Second, it can be trouble matching the shape and size of the stone with the shape and size of the bezel cup. Purchased cups can only be found in a limited number of standard sizes. You may have to adjust your choice of gemstone to match the cup.

A second consideration is that pre-made cups often have fairly low side walls. While these are fine for low-dome stones, they're not dependable for stones with steep side walls.

Lastly before setting, check the fit of your gemstone in the cup, particularly around the bottom. The bottom corners of a stamped cup are much more rounded than a bezel you would fabricate yourself. This causes a problem with stones that have a sharp edge around the bottom. Burnishing the bezel over one of these stones will place a lot of stress on the stone and may cause it to crack. To avoid this, I round off the bottom edge of the stone with a diamond file (or use sandpaper on soft stones).

RAISING A CABOCHON

When a cabochon sits too low in a bezel, the bezel hides a lot of the stone. The solution is to either sand down the bezel height or boost up the stone. If you choose to raise it up, what is the best material to use?

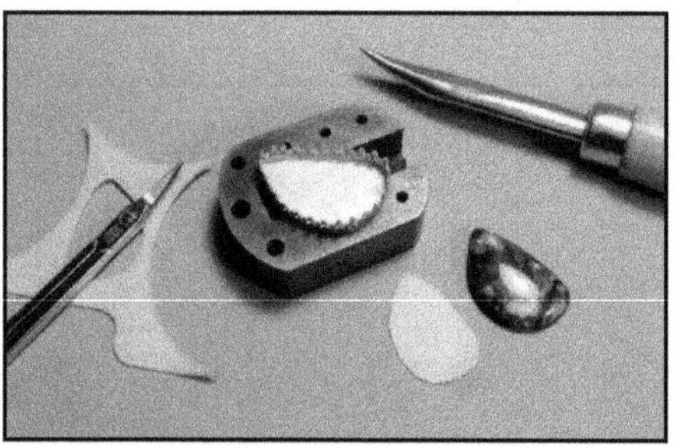

I was taught to use fine sawdust but now think that might be a problem when used in rings. I reason that rings will frequently get wet, which would cause the sawdust to swell in size and push the stone against the bezel. Then when the sawdust dries out, the stone would be a little loose.

Using pieces of plastic sheet is a better solution. Plastic is readily available from product packaging or from old credit cards. Cut a piece to loosely fit the bezel, and drop in the stone (with some dental floss) to check its height.

REMOVING EXCESS SOLDER

Sometimes when you solder a bezel to a base plate, you end up with excess solder that needs to be removed before setting the stone. My choice of a tool bit for this is called an "Inverse Cone" bur used in a rotary tool or flexshaft. It cuts on both the bottom and the side, and it is shaped so that there's less chance of cutting into the bezel wall than if I used the more common cylinder bur shape. I find a 2-3 mm size useful for most bezels.

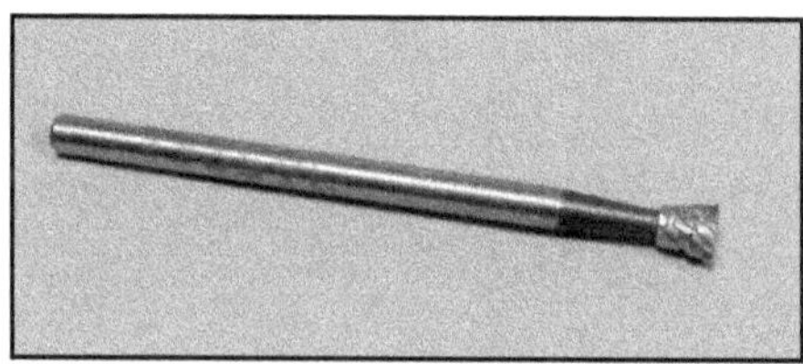

TRANSPARENT CABS

When bezel setting a transparent cabochon in silver, I worry that the silver will tarnish under the stone and will destroy the brilliance of its color and pattern. So I take one extra step before setting the stone. I place a piece of thin silver Mylar plastic under the stone to act as a mirror that will never tarnish.

Mylar is readily available in craft and gift wrap stores, or in a pinch, from a party balloon supplier. You can also experiment with using colored or patterned Mylar (i.e. diffraction pattern) under some stones.

WHEN BEZELS SHRINK

The engineer in me says there's no reason a bezel should shrink when I solder it onto a base plate. But sometimes I find that the stone won't quite fit into the bezel that was perfect just before soldering.

If that ever happens to you, here's a fix that usually works for those times when there's just a minor problem. I file or sand the stone down a little around its base. For soft cabs like turquoise, lapis, jet or Howlite, a sanding stick can be used. For harder cabs like jaspers or agates, a diamond file will be required.

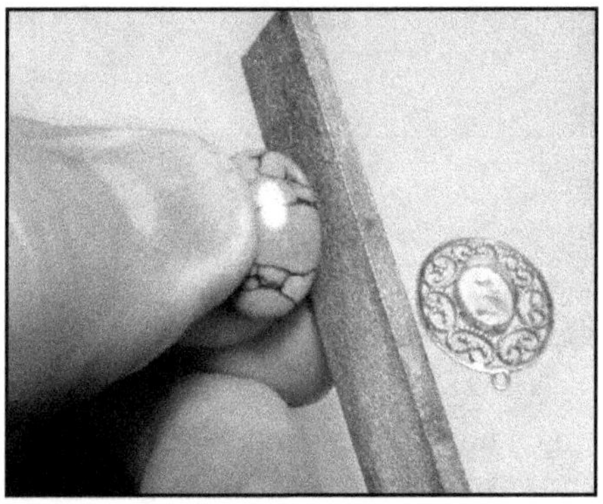

There are two important things to remember when doing this. First, you can only make a minor adjustment to the stone's size. All filing or sanding has to be hidden by the bezel because it takes the polish off the stone.

Secondly, remember to round off all sharp edges on the bottom of the stone. A sharp edge here might sit on a little extra solder that's in the bottom joint of the bezel. A little bump of solder can put enough stress on the stone to risk breakage when the bezel is burnished down on the stone.

CHAPTER 8

TOOLS TIPS

BALL BURS

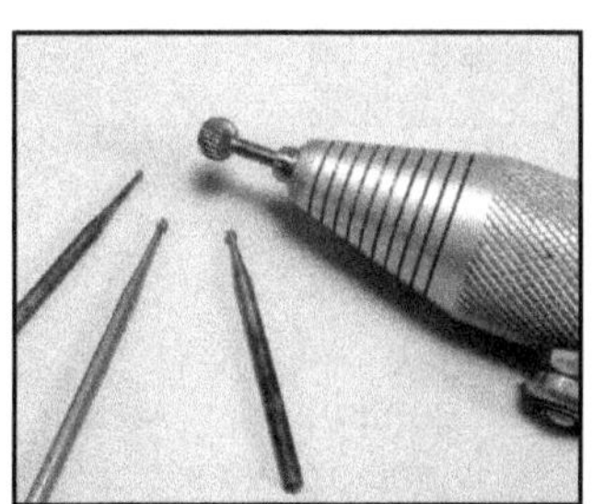

I use ball burs quite a bit for carving and for cutting off bits of excess solder. The ball shape seems to be more controllable than other cutting burs. They're less apt to grab and walk over your piece.

As for sizes, I've found that 8 mm is a very useful size for carving while a 1/2 mm or smaller at high speed works great for signing your name on the back of your work.

BENCH SHEARS

When cutting sheet metal, it's quicker and easier to use a set of shop shears as compared with using a hand saw. The cut is not as precise, but many times you don't need that. Shears will easily cut up to 24 gauge sheet, and some will cut 22 or even 20 gauge.

Current prices for shears run up to $22 in jewelry catalogs, and the Joyce Chen scissors recommended on some jewelry blogs are usually more than that. But I found a cheaper alternative at the 99 Cent Store - gardening utility scissors for only $1.07.

I buy a half dozen of them at a time for use in my jewelry classes. They're great for cutting bezels, trimming around a bezel cup, and cutting a piece off a larger sheet.

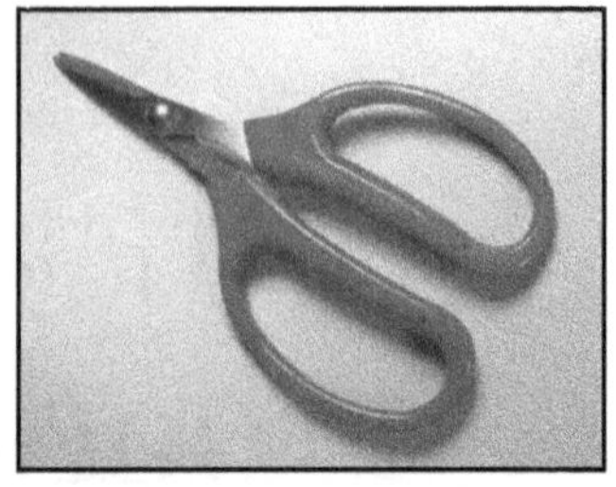

BEZEL CLOSER

A bezel closer is a steel punch that makes quick work out of pushing the metal down over a round stone and burnishing it. It works with regular bezels, with tube settings, and with prong settings. Stones can be set in as little as 30 seconds.

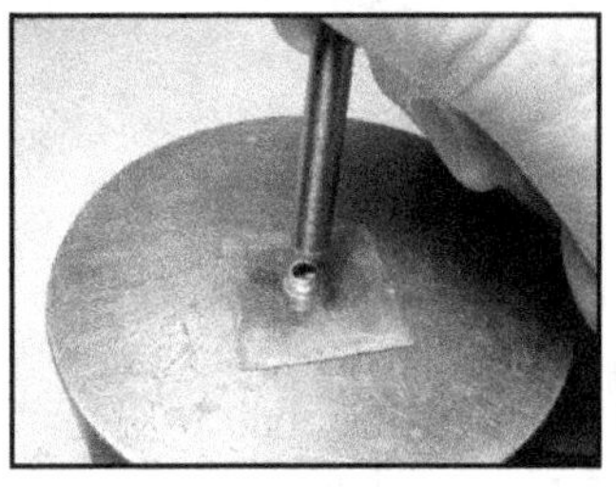

The working end is a concave cavity that fits over a bezel or prong setting and is pushed and twisted to capture the stone. Sets can be purchased but are quite expensive and contain many sizes you will probably never use. If all you need is one or two sizes, here's how you can make them yourself.

Find a good quality, round steel rod a little larger in diameter than the bezel cup or prong setting. Cut a 5 inch length. File both ends flat. Locate the center of one end, centerpunch a divot, and drill a small pilot hole about 5 mm deep. Remember to use a little oil as lubricant.

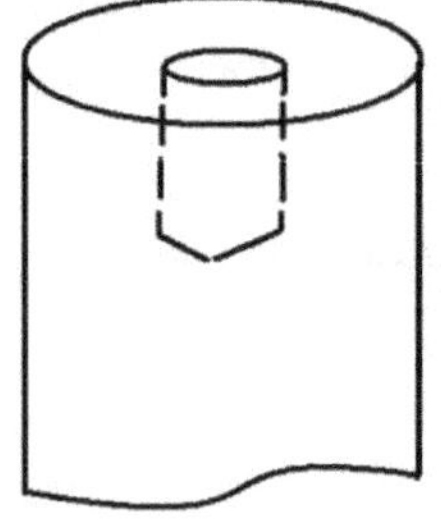

Select a ball bur a bit smaller than the steel rod but slightly larger than the bezel. Enlarge the pilot hole to a full hemispherical cavity. Test for proper fit with your bezel. The bezel should first contact the cavity about a third of the way in. When the size is correct, polish the cavity using Zam on a length of chopstick in your flexshaft. If the tool is not polished, it will leave scratches on your bezel or prongs.

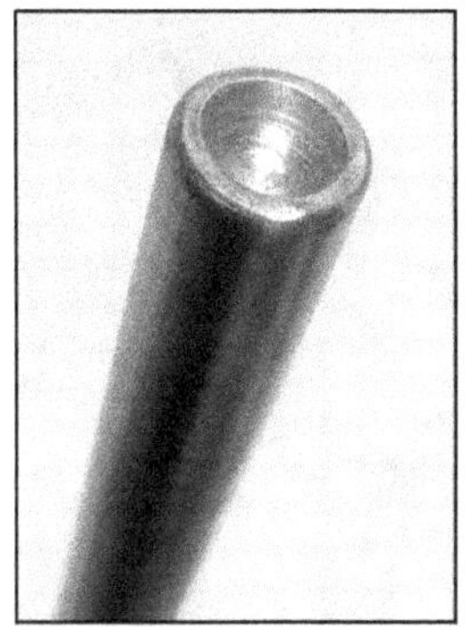

When using the tool, the first step is to capture the stone correctly. I usually work by hand and push the punch straight down over the bezel or prongs. This causes the metal to start bending over the stone. Next, if it's a small stone, I inspect with a lens to be sure the stone is staying level. This is repeated until the stone is seated on its bearing and can't move anymore.

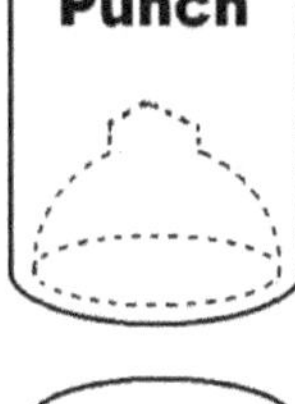

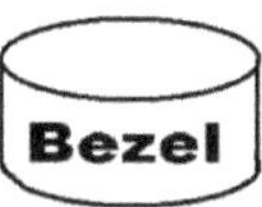

Next, you want to force the metal down onto the stone uniformly all the way around. While this can be done by hand, I often gently tap the punch with a hammer. Finally, I burnish the bezel by twisting the punch around.

CUTTING MOLDS

Cutting molds is easier and more precise with a sharp blade. A new Xacto blade is sufficient for cutting RTV molds but is not sharp enough for vulcanized rubber. For that it's best to use scalpel blades available from most jewelry supply companies. The #11 blade is triangle shaped, and the #12 is hawksbill shaped. I find the hawksbill is handy for cutting the registration keys.

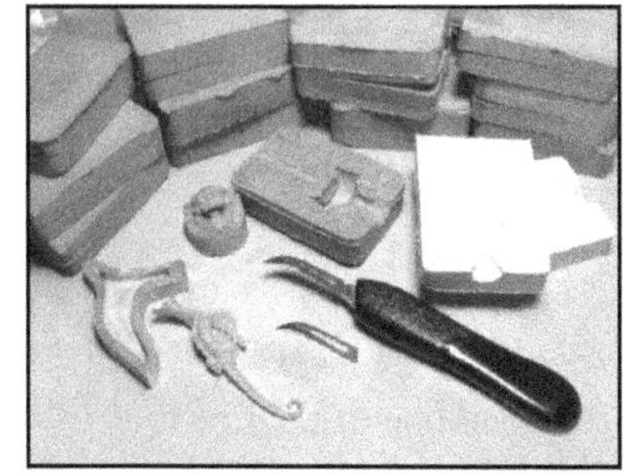

CUTOFF WHEELS

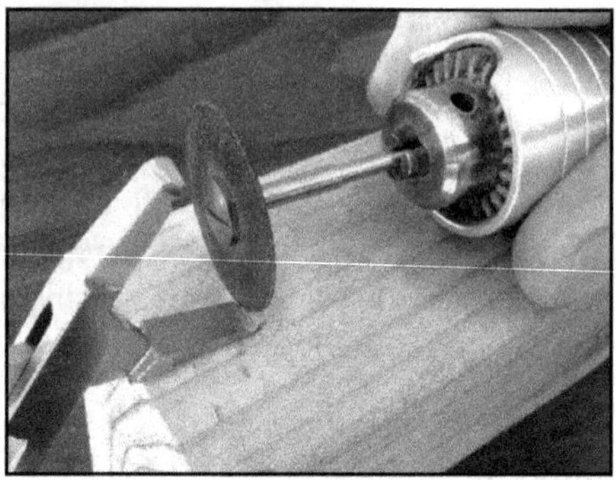

Cutoff wheels (also called Separating Discs) are inexpensive and do a great job grinding steel. They can be used to sharpen tool points, cut piano wire to length, make slots, and sharpen worn drills. Other uses include modifying pliers and making your own design stamps.

My preference is the 1 inch diameter size. Be sure to hold the wheel firmly so nothing moves to break the disc, and definitely wear safety glasses. A flake of steel in caught in your eye makes for a bad day.

DENTAL TOOLS

A ready source of free tools is your local dentist. Dental picks can be reworked into wax tools or straightened and sharpened to make a stylus for marking and layout. The steel in these tools is high quality, and the handles are designed for comfort.

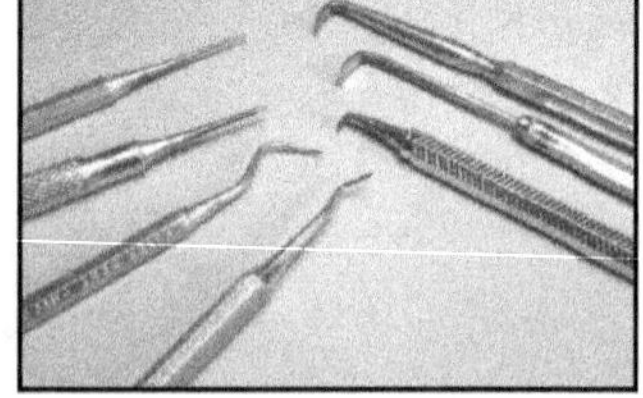

A special note however - don't try to bend one of the tips to a different shape - the steel will snap. To change the shape, heat the tip to red hot and bend it with pliers while it's hot.

And don't forget to ask your dentist for some of the cutting burs they throw out. These are useful for a variety of things. It's best to call a week or two before your visit to ask the dentist to save some of these tools for you. It's good practice also to ask that they run them through the sterilizer. If that's not possible, pop them in an oven at around 250 F

LAYOUT TOOLS

Dimensions on some features of a design can be fluid while others must be accurate for the design to work. When precision on a piece is important, good layout techniques are essential. These are the tools that I rely upon to get holes in the right place, to achieve correct angles, and to cut pieces the correct length.

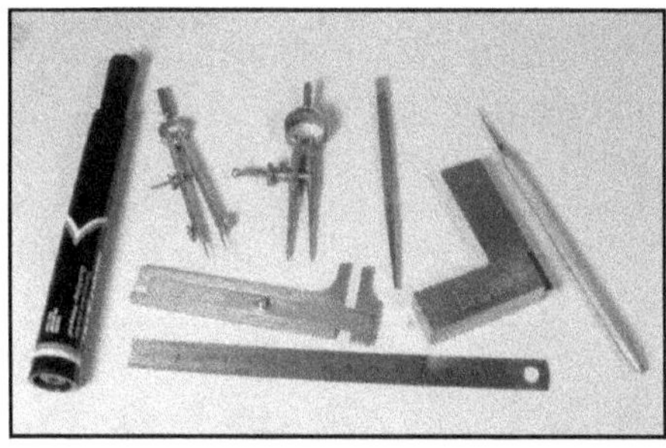

I like crisp sharp lines to follow, so I often coat surfaces with a dark marker and scribe my layout lines onto the metal. A square makes quick work of checking right angles or marking where to cut, and the thin centerpunch helps me mark a place to drill holes exactly where I want them.

Finally, a good set of dividers are probably my favorite layout tool. They quickly mark a strip for cutting, can swing an arc, and can divide a line or curve into as many equal segments as needed. I keep at least one set of dividers in every toolbox.

MARKING YOUR TOOLS

It makes sense to mark your tools if you ever lend them to friends or take them out to classes or workshops. Question is how to mark them permanently. For metal tools, I use a very small ball bur running fast in the Dremel or Foredom to "engrave" my initials. Other times I'll form the initials with a number of hits with a center punch.

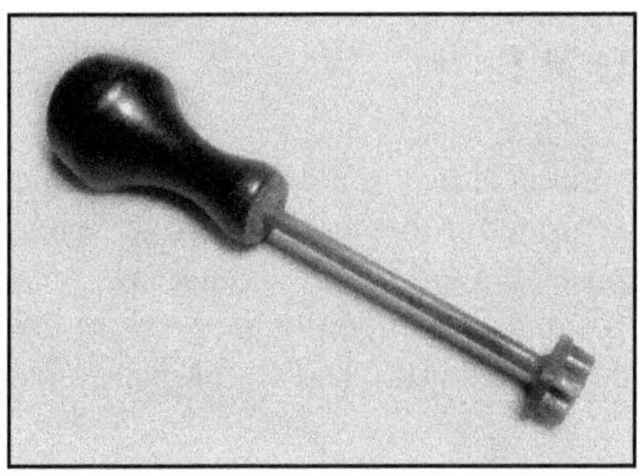

But for hammer handles and other wooden tools, the country boy in me thought of a branding iron. If you'd like to try one, all that's needed is a little scrap copper or nickel, about 22-24 gauge, a piece of heavy brass or copper for a base, about six inches of metal rod, and a piece of wood for the handle.

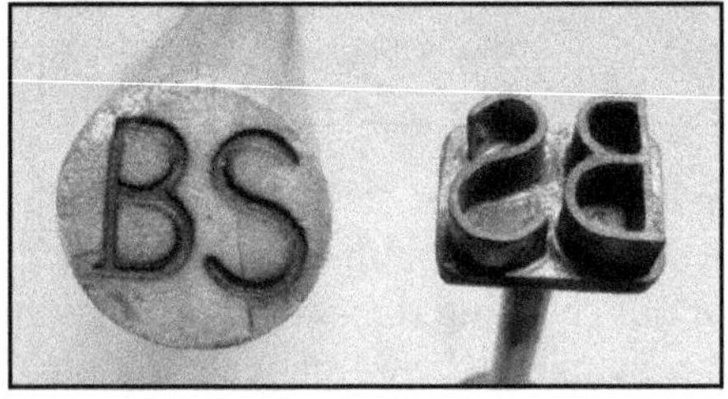

I formed my initials from a couple 4mm strips of sheet nickel. The "S" was one piece, but the "B" was three pieces soldered together with hard. Remember to form the letters backwards. Then solder the letters with medium onto a piece of 1/8 inch thick brass bar to act as a heat sink.

NO - MAR PLIERS

Pliers can often leave nicks and scratches on your work. If this is a problem, first take a close look at the pliers jaws. New tools can be a little rough. I typically relieve any sharp edges, sand away any tool marks, and give working areas a quick polish.

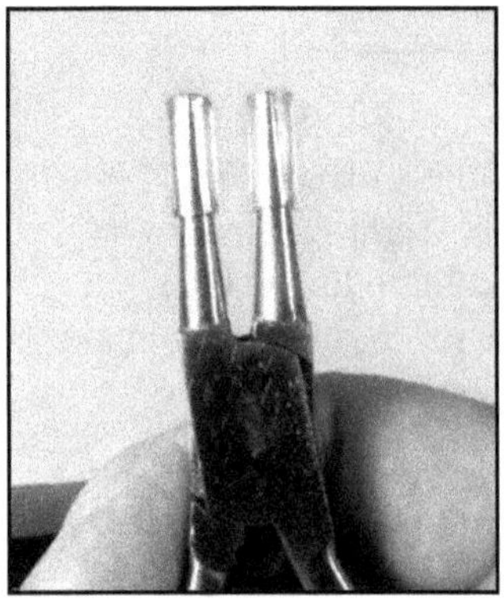

If that doesn't solve the problem, you probably need to cover the jaws. Plastic electrical tape provides a quick fix but can leave messy adhesive on the jaws. Dips don't seem to last very long. A quick and easy way I've found is to slip a length of 1/8 dia vinyl tubing over each jaw. The tubing can be found in a store that sells aquarium supplies.

It works well, fast, and leaves no sticky residue. The only problem is that it increases the size of the pliers jaws a bit.

TEMPLATES

Whenever I have to make more than 2-3 exact copies of anything, I think of making a template. A template lets me easily draw the shape of an item. Art stores sell templates for common shapes like circles, ovals, hearts, etc. Other sources would include Cool Tools and Kingsley North.

For non standard shapes, it's easy to make your own template. Simply cut the shape out of sheet plastic or thin sheet metal. My preference is brass. I carefully lay out the shape using a steel ruler, a set of dividers, a scribe, and a fine center punch.

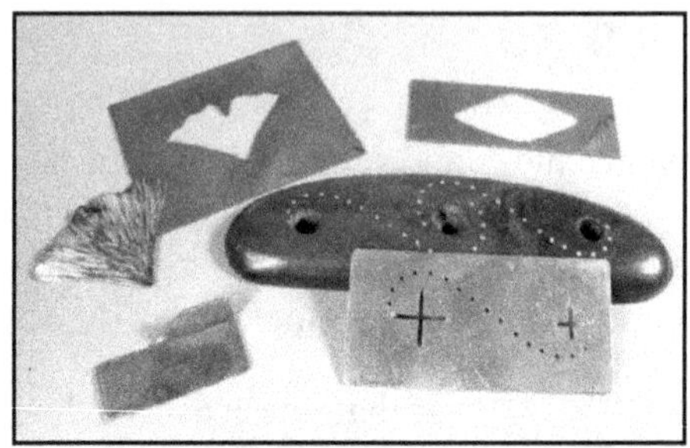

One example is the brass template in the upper-left that lets me quickly trace the design of a ginkgo leaf onto silver sheet. Another is the nickel template in the lower-right that makes it easy to drill a pattern of holes for pin inlay into the wooden handle. Templates save a lot of time whenever you have to make multiples or make a symmetrical pattern.

TRY A TOOTHPICK

The round, stronger wooden toothpicks have a multitude of uses in the jewelry shop. I use them for things like mixing epoxy resin, applying paste solder, and polishing in tight spots with Zam or rouge.

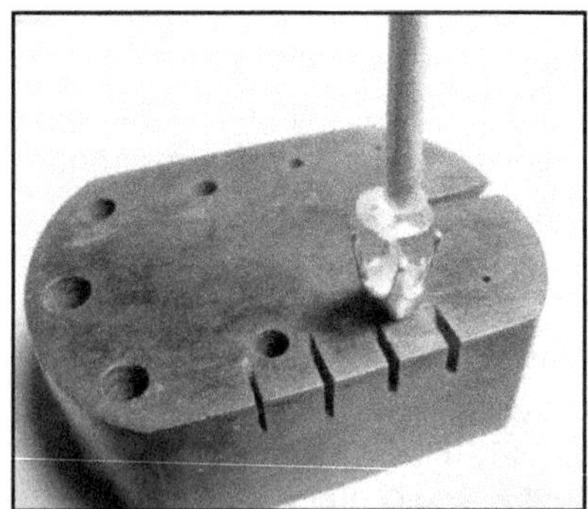

Toothpicks are quite handy when testing the fit of a small faceted stone in a prong or tube setting. Just break off the sharp tip, mold a little beeswax over it, and press it onto the table of your stone to make a nice handle.

CHAPTER 9

EQUIPMENT TIPS

ADJUSTABLE CHUCK

Many of us have a Dremel motor tool to use at home or when out to a class or workshop. The one thing that makes this tool much more productive is the addition of one inexpensive option - an adjustable chuck.

The motor tool as sold typically comes with a collet chuck. This means you have to use a wrench to change every tool bit, you have to switch collets to use different shaft sizes (3/32 inch or 1/8 inch bits), and ordinary drills can't be used at all - only the special ones that have a 3/32 shaft.

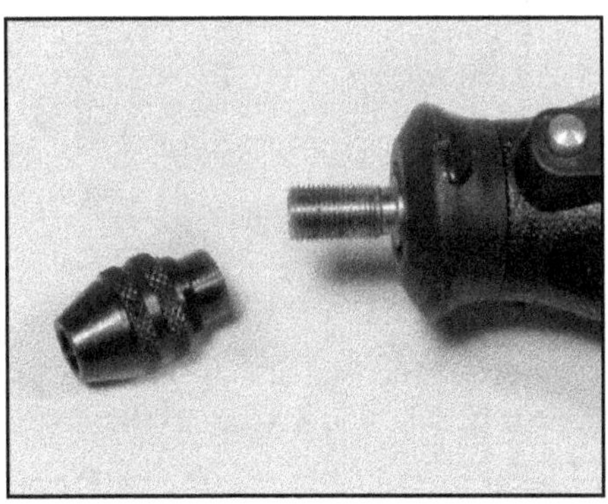

A simple and inexpensive adjustable chuck solves all of these problems. It's available for Dremels in most large local hardware stores or at model making outlets. Tightening the chuck is done easily by hand to any small size shaft.

No wrench or key is required with this kind of chuck.

ELECTRIC WAX PEN

You can make your own wax pen from a small soldering iron plugged into a light dimmer switch for heat control. Both components are easily found at a big hardware store or at Harbor Freight. As an example of the components, see items # 43060 and # 47887 at www.harborfreight.com

Look for a soldering iron of around 25-30 watts. File the tip to the shape you prefer, or get a soldering iron with replaceable tips. Then you can make several tip shapes for different tasks. Set the dimmer control just hot enough to melt the wax without producing any smoke.

FLEXSHAFT STAND

A quick and easy way to suspend a flexshaft over your jewelry bench is to use some steel pipe components from your local hardware store. It attaches with a couple screws and only costs about $10.

I use 1/2 inch galvanized pipe and fittings. To build a stand that attaches onto the top of your bench, all you'll need is a flange and a 30 inch pipe.

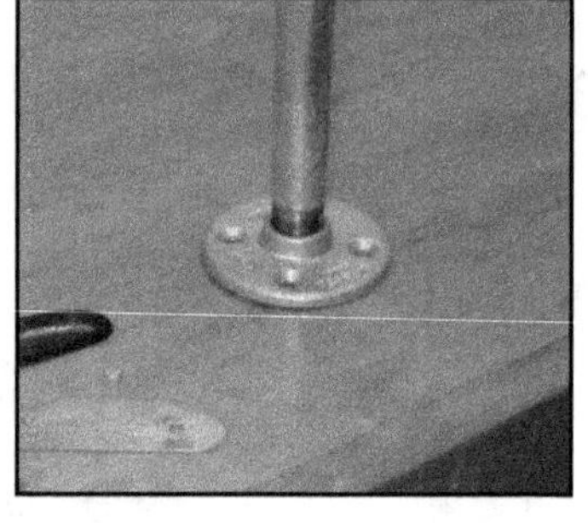

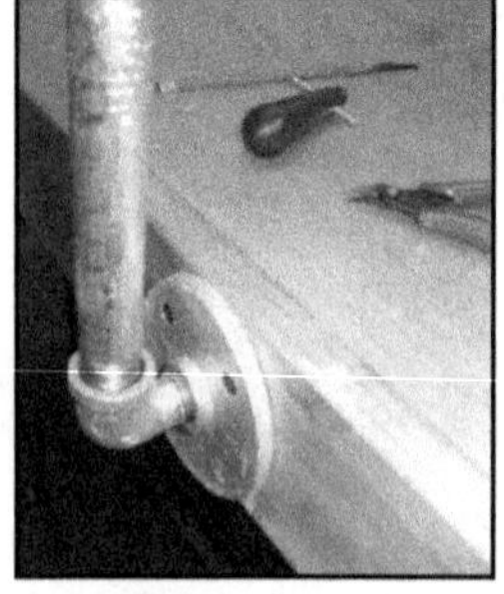

If you prefer a stand that attaches to the side of your bench, you'll need a little longer pipe, perhaps three foot, a flange, and a 90 degree "street elle".

To complete the Foredom stand, make a hook out of heavy gauge steel or aluminum rod to hang the motor from the top of the pipe. Heavy coat hanger wire works well, or 1/8 inch rod is available at most hardware stores.

HOMEMADE WAX TOOLS

Used X-Acto or scalpel blades can be repurposed for numerous jobs on the workbench. For instance, they're wonderful for wax work. A cutoff wheel or other type of grinding wheel shapes them quickly.

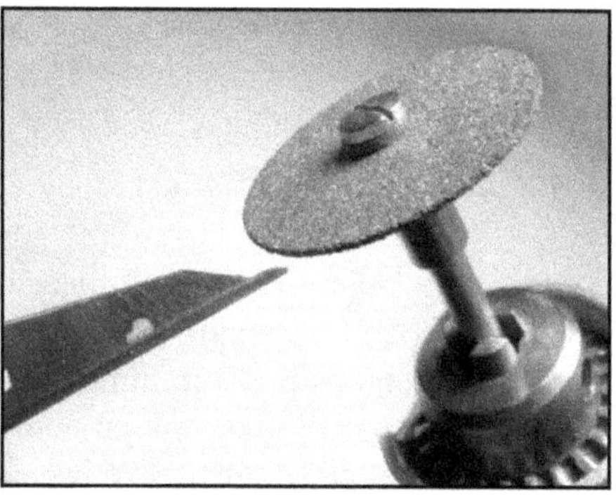

Here I'm carving away excess metal on the spine of the blade to make a narrow carving knife that does a great job detailing small pierced areas on your waxes.

Blades can also be bent to make scrapers for sculpting surfaces or cutting grooves with a flat, curved or V-shaped bottom. First shape the end of the blade to the width and geometry you need. Then use a torch to heat the blade to red before bending it with pliers. Sharpened blades can be hardened by quenching and tempering, but that is not usually necessary when working with soft materials like waxes.

FOREDOM MAINTENANCE

If you have a Foredom flexshaft, it makes sense to check it over every so often to be sure it's running properly. But how to do that? Well, being the good company it is, Foredom has put together an extensive set of videos on how to do it.

The series covers set-up, lubrication, replacing a sheath, motor maintenance, and handpiece maintenance. Few if any special tools are needed. You can watch the videos at www.foredom.net/flexibleshaftmachinemaintenance.aspx particularly under "Foredom Basics" or the "Foredom Shafting..." categories. Any repair parts needed are available on the Foredom site or from most jewelry supply catalogs.

MINI DRILL PRESS

If you find yourself drilling a number of small holes in your work, you might want to look at the small, inexpensive drill presses now available. They take up just minimal space on the bench and are always ready to drill nice straight holes. Some models even have a variable speed control. I've been very pleased with a low-priced one that's been well-used in my classes for over a year.

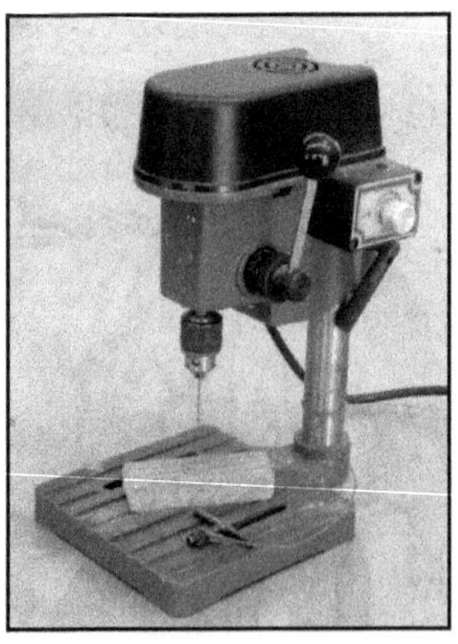

Because these machines are only a foot high, they're limited as to the size of workpieces that can fit into the machine and the size of the drill bits you can use. But I've had no problems with drill bits up to about 3/16 inch (4.5mm), even drilling steel. The machines are sold by a number of companies. If you do get one, be sure to buy a spare belt because they are generally not available at local hardware stores.

REVOLVING SOLDER PAD

Often when we're soldering, we have multiple pieces on the pad or a single piece and would like to work on several sides of it during the same heat. One of the ways to deal with this is to put a solder pad onto a turntable. That way you can rotate each piece into position when needed or easily rotate the pad to reach another side of a larger piece.

All that's needed to make one of these is a piece of aluminum sheet and an inexpensive turntable assembly. A good hardware store should have both. Aluminum sheet can also be found in the scrap pile of a local sheet metal shop.

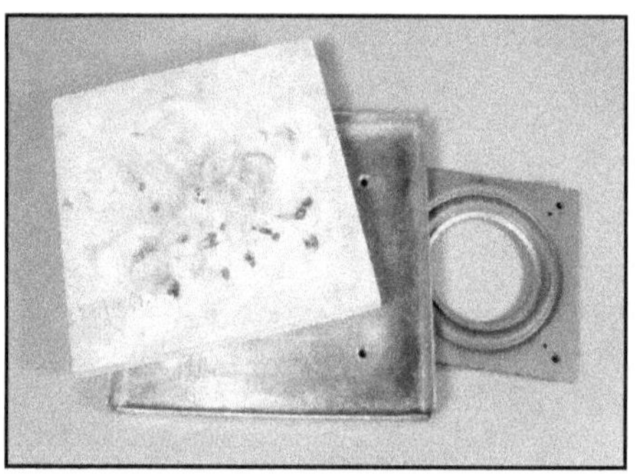

In building a turntable for a six inch square solder pad, I used a seven inch square piece of aluminum and cut out 1/2 inch notches from each corner. I used a bench vise to bend the sides along the dotted lines to form a tray that cradles the solder pad. The tray is attached to the turntable unit with 4 machine screws.

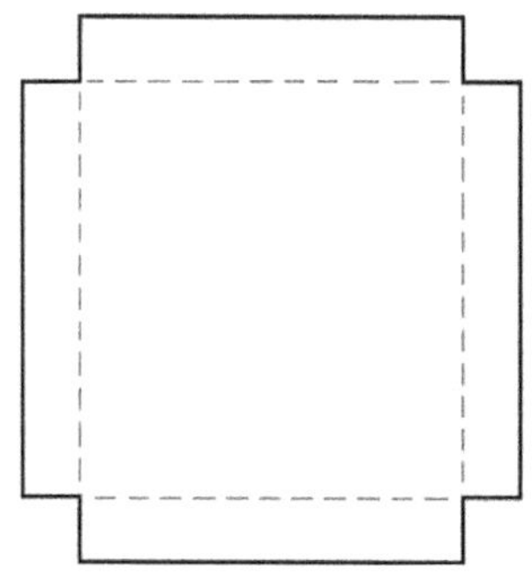

CHAPTER 10

SAFETY TIPS

DRILLING SMALL ITEMS

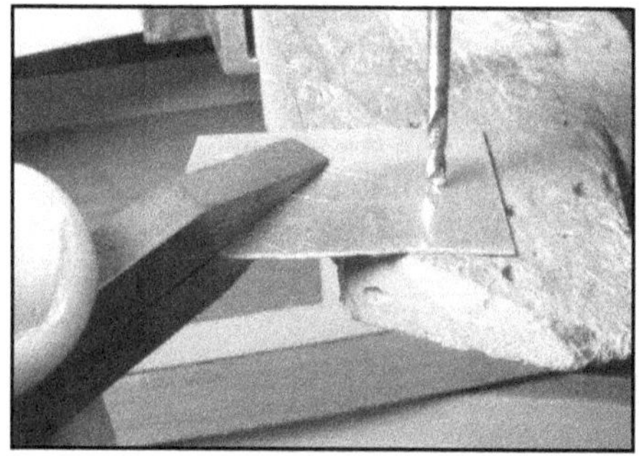

Small pieces need to be held securely while drilling to prevent them from spinning if the drill catches. Having sliced my fingers occasionally in my younger days, I avoid band-aids now by using flat-jaw pliers or a ring clamp. Pliers also save your fingers if the piece gets hot. Put a little tape over plier jaws if needed to avoid scratches.

DRILL PRESS VISE

A drill press vise is a versatile tool to hold a workpiece securely and in precise alignment. It reduces the risks of working with high-power motors, use of larger drill bits, and higher heat generated in the operation. The vise can be clamped to the drill press table if needed and is quite handy for bench use to hold things for sawing or riveting.

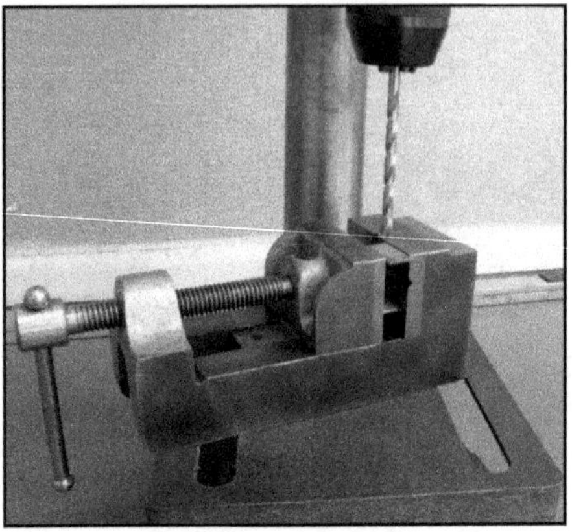

Vises can be found in stores that specialize in machine tool supplies. My feeling is that the best ones are made from steel. In particular, a nice feature on some designs are the V grooves cut into the jaw plates. They let me securely hold a punch straight upright or hold a rod perfectly horizontal.

LITTLE THINGS CAN BITE

Most jewelers treat motorized equipment with caution. We've all heard stories about workpieces coming loose in the drill press or about getting long hair or clothing caught in the polishing machine. It stands to reason that a machine with a motor of a 1/3 horsepower or so is going to win out over its operator. We all know that, and I'm not going to harp on it. That's not the point of this story.

I want to talk about the smaller motor-powered machines we often use, the ones with small three inch diameter motors such as used in flexshafts and micro buffers. Many of us forget caution when using them, but they can get you into trouble. Here's what happened to two people I know.

One friend had a polishing bur bend in the handpiece and whack her thumb so badly that it seemed the bone might have been broken. The swelling was substantial, and it took a couple weeks to regain normal use. A small underpowered motor? I don't think so.

Another friend was using one of the small buffing machines, the kind you can stop when you apply a little too much pressure to the wheel. Not to worry about such an underpowered beast you say. Wrong, it literally jumped up and bit the hand that feeds it!

The buffer was set on a low table to do a quick polish, so was not mounted or clamped. A buff was installed on the right spindle, no buff on the left. Friend was wearing a tight-fitting, long-sleeved sweater. While buffing on the right wheel, the left tapered spindle caught a thread on the friend's left sleeve and started grabbing more and more threads and sleeve.

Rather than pulling the arm into the machine, the light buffer quickly lifted off the table and started climbing up the underside of my friend's arm. There was no way to get a hand of the on/off switch because the unit was spinning wildly and battering her like a club wielded by a mad man. Only when she could grab the gyrating power cord and yank it from the wall did the mayhem stop.

So when you're in the shop, please think safety. Don't take even those little motors for granted.

PICKLE PRECAUTIONS

A hot pickle pot gives off acid fumes that bother me in my home workshop. I get around that by using my pickle cold. I mix it a little stronger than for a hot pot so that it works almost as quickly. I keep it in a large-mouth plastic bottle and cap it off whenever I'm done using it.

LOOSE HEADS

Flying off the handle is never good, particularly if it's a hammer head. The traditional way to tighten a loose hammer head is a bit of work with wedges, but if the head is basically secure, there's a fast and easy way to tighten a loose head for about 50 cents - superglue.

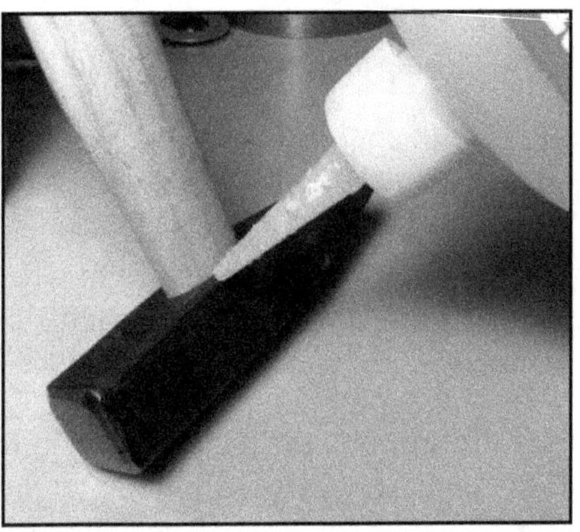

Simply put a couple drops in from the handle side, let it set up, and then a few drops in from the top side. Be sure to get the thin superglue, not gel. It penetrates better. Packages of two superglues are usually available at the 99 Cent Store.

Note that this is only a safe practice if the hammer head is just a little loose and is basically secured onto the handle. Gluing is not a fix for a hammer head that has come off the handle or is at risk of coming off.

LOWERING THE NOISE

A simple way to cut down the noise when you're hammering on your small anvil or bench block is to place it on an old mouse pad or other similar rubber material.

RISKS OF NATURAL GAS

Some jewelers in the USA are tapping in to their natural gas system to fuel their torch. Two students have asked me if this was safe. Because I'm not an expert in torch gas systems I called the engineering department of Smith Equipment Company and tech support at Rio Grande. Both told me it was not safe to use natural gas available in US homes.

The problem concerns a thing called a flashback arrestor that isolates your torch from the sources of oxygen and fuel gas. The people at both Smith (605 882-3200) and Rio (800 545-6566) explained that home natural gas comes in at too low a pressure for the flashback arrestor to function correctly. This means that a problem at the torch could propagate a fire back through the fuel hose and into your home's gas pipe system. That can't be good.

Natural gas pressure in a U.S. home is typically about one-quarter of one pound per square inch, very low. Flashback arrestors require at least two pounds per square inch to work properly. Special equipment is available to solve the problem, but it is quite expensive.

So it's best to use bottled fuel gas through a regulator and flashback arrestor.

My jewelry bench is inside my home, not in a garage or a separate shop building, so I'm obviously concerned that the operation is safe. On the advice of a local fire marshal, I do not use a refillable fuel gas tank. He said it contains too much gas in case of a leak and would be a problem with my home insurance.

So my choice of fuel gas is to use propane in 14 ounce disposable cylinders. I use it with a refillable oxygen tank that, like medical oxygen, is quite safe for use in the house.

QUENCHING

Some jewelers drop the hot piece from soldering directly into the pickle. Hear that little hiss? The hot piece sends small droplets of acid into the air. This can rust nearby tools and can't be all that good to breathe either. To avoid this I quench in water. A coffee cup of water at the solder station lets you cool a soldered piece before dumping it into the pickle. It's also useful for annealing metals and for cooling off tweezers.

CHAPTER 11

MISCELLANEOUS TIPS

FAKES & FRAUDS

I'm fortunate to live in a big city with frequent jewelry shows where I can buy supplies. But there are certain risks in buying at one of these events. Recently, a friend bought a package of 12 mm Sterling jump rings that became copper-plated in the pickle. There was no sign of any steel contamination, so I tested them with a magnet to discover they were plated steel.

Best solution is to carry a couple simple tools with you when you go to buy stones or findings. I usually take a ten power loupe and a small vernier caliper to measure things. From now on, I'll also be carrying a small, strong magnet as well.

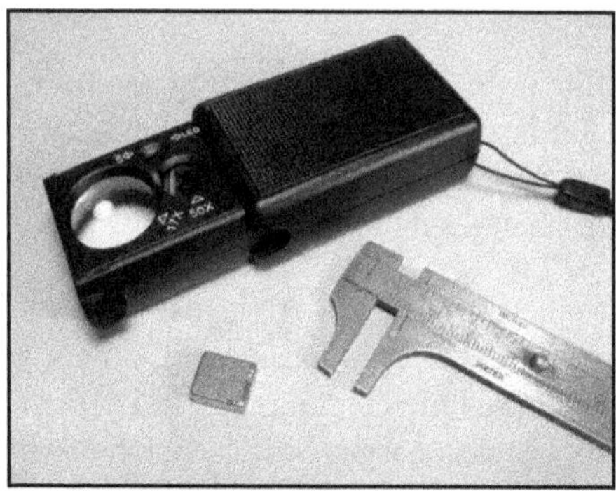

Dealers are not necessarily the problem. Many have no idea their metals are plated. They were duped by their supplier.

JUMP RING WEAR

It's better to use a round jump ring on the end of a chain instead of an oval one. Oval rings will wear faster because tension on the chain concentrates wear on the smaller ends of the jump ring. Wear is distributed evenly on a round jump ring because it can rotate through the last link of the chain and the clasp. This gives the ring a longer useful life.

INVENTORY RECORD

In an ideal world, each of us has a complete pictorial record of all pieces of jewelry in our inventory. We use it for insurance. We use it as a record of what was sent out on consignment. We use it to remember which items we are taking to a show. And eventually, we use it as a record of what we have sold.

Unfortunately, we don't always have time to take good pictures for the inventory. In situations like this, I've been able to make a quick record with the help of a color copier. Simply place a number of pieces face down on the glass and make a copy. The quality is more than sufficient for an accurate record.

SAVE ON SILVER

Silver products like sheet, wire, and casting shot are sold by the Troy ounce at what is called the spot price. That's what companies pay for the pure metal on the commodities market, and the spot price changes daily.

But in addition to the spot price, there is also a cost to fabricate the metal into wire or sheet, so the price of the item you buy is the cost of the metal plus the cost to make it. Different products have different fabrication charges because each takes a different amount of labor. Also, different companies will have different fabrication charges because of local labor rates and their desired profit margin.

Save money by finding a company with a lower fabrication charge. Also, note that the fabrication charge per ounce is less on larger orders, so you can save more by buying more. Find a friend to place a joint order and split the shipping charges.

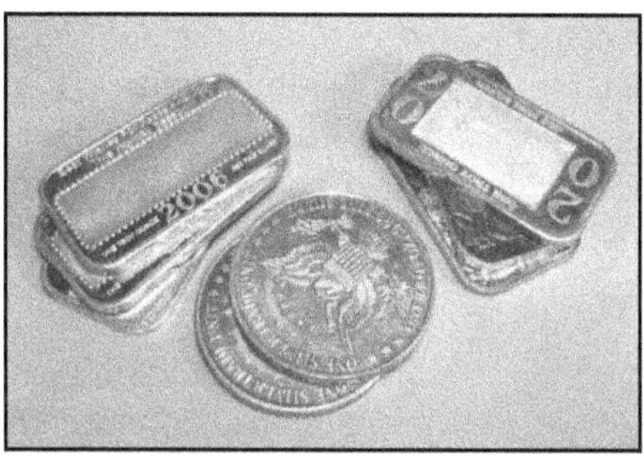

But for casting purposes, there's an even better way to save. Buy your silver at a local coin store. They sell bars and rounds in pure and Sterling for the spot price plus about a dollar per ounce.

Coin shops have no fabrication charge and charge just a small profit over the spot price. Further, they may waive the sales tax on a cash buy. So I save about $3 per ounce, pay no tax, no shipping charges, and support a local business.

TAKE A BETTER PHOTO

Most digital cameras these days have the ability to take a good picture of your small jewelry items, but set-up is important. There are four major items to control - background, lighting, camera motion, and focus control.

Lightly colored papers from an art store make reasonable starter backgrounds. Avoid fabrics because the weave can often be distracting at high magnification.

Outside lighting is the easiest. In fact for close-ups, flash never works well. Turn off your camera's flash. Choose a bright but overcast day or a lightly shaded area when the sun is full. For inside photos, two gooseneck desk lamps can be used with 75 watt bulbs. Whatever you use, be sure to set the camera to match the type of lighting you use or else the colors will be off.

You'll be shooting up close, so turn on the Macro mode. Now at this range, if the camera moves even a little bit during the shot, the picture will be blurry, so it's essential to use a tripod. Used ones are available inexpensively from eBay, yard sales, or some camera shops. And even with a tripod, I put the camera on the self-timer mode so that any vibration from clicking the button settles down before the camera takes a picture.

In order to get the largest part of your jewelry in focus, you need to close the lens down to the minimum aperture (highest F-Stop number). This is done by taking the camera off of "Auto" mode and selecting Aperture Priority, usually denoted by "Av", and then setting the aperture to the largest number, which is F-8 on my camera. Get out the camera operation book if necessary, or go back to the store and ask how to do this. It's really worth the effort.

That's it. In recap, here are the camera settings I use:

Set the lens to Macro for a close-up shot.

Turn the camera's flash off.

Move the camera in close enough for the item to cover at least ¾ of the frame.

Look for adverse reflections from the jewelry surface.

Try to minimize reflections with changes of light position, camera angle, or white background paper.

Carefully check for any fingerprints or dust that might be on the piece.

Make any final tweaks with light and arrangement.

Select "Av" for aperture priority mode.

Set the lens opening to the highest number for maximum depth of field.

Set the lighting to match what you're using (daylight, overcast, lightbulb, fluorescent, etc).

Set the timer to delayed shooting, either 2 seconds or 10 seconds, to avoid camera movement. The delay also gives you time to hold up a piece of white paper to reduce any final reflections.

Set the image size to the maximum resolution. You can size it down later, but you can never increase it.

Take the shot.

WHAT A NICE PIECE

You're wearing one of the pieces you've made, and someone compliments it. What do you say?

It's always polite to thank the person. But if that's all you do, you're missing out on a great sales opportunity. Even if you're not actively selling your work, some good public relations is always worthwhile.

If someone notices a piece you're wearing, you should have a short sentence or two memorized to take maximum advantage of the moment..What you say could be as simple as:

"Thanks. I make my own jewelry. Here's my card."

A FAVOR PLEASE

Reviews are a significant way for books to gain visibility. As an independent author, I hope you enjoyed

Bench Tips for Jewelry Making

and I'd truly appreciate it if you could post a few words of review on Amazon

amazon.com/dp/0988285800

- Thank you

ABOUT THE AUTHOR

Brad Smith is a studio jeweler, lapidary, and jewelry instructor in Santa Monica, CA. He enjoys working with silver, gold, exotic woods, bone, fossil ivory, and meteorite.

As a long-time member of the Culver City Rock Club, Brad has taught lapidary skills, led field trips to the Mojave Desert, organized gem and mineral shows, and held many positions, including club President. He is a member of the Metal Arts Society of Southern California where he served as Vice President and on the Board of Directors. There he organized workshops with nationally known jewelry artists.

His teaching career started with the Los Angeles school system where he taught Advanced Jewelry in the Adult Education Department for eight years. In 2009, he designed and built a new jewelry facility at Santa Monica's Adult Education Center where he currently teaches beginning and advanced classes.

Brad also likes photography, develops websites, and moderates several jewelry making and rockhounding discussion groups on the Internet.

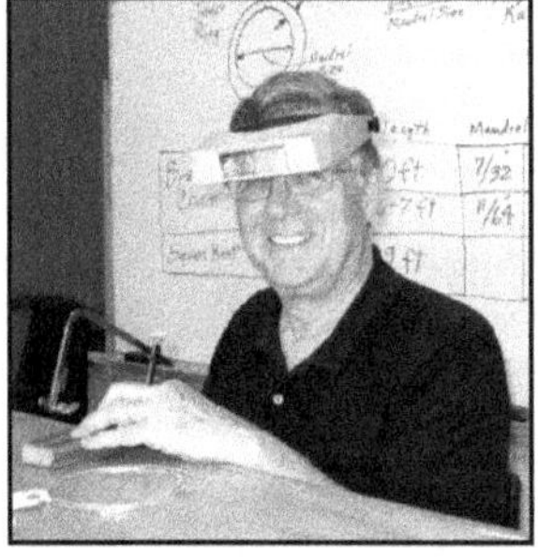

Contact the author at <benchtips@yahoo.com>

http://www.BradSmithJewelry.com

OTHER BOOKS BY THE AUTHOR

Accessories for the Foredom and Dremel

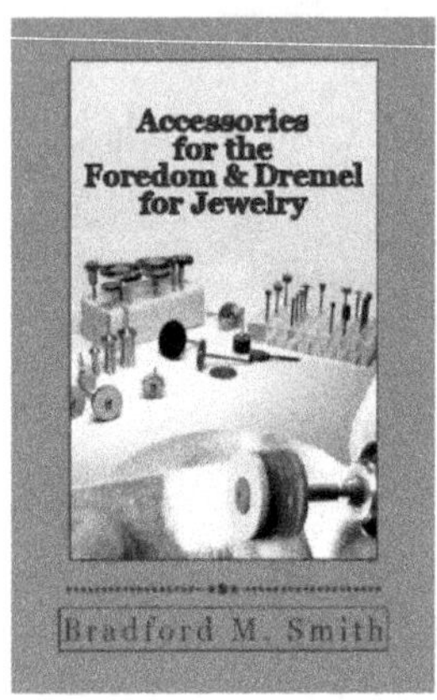

Flexible shaft and Dremels are an indispensable help to those who make jewelry, improving both the productivity and the quality of work. But with such an array of different tool bits to choose from, it's sometimes difficult to figure out which bits to use.

"Accessories for the Foredom and Dremel" surveys the range of tool bits available for use with flexible shaft and hand-held motor tools and discusses the merits of each.

It highlights the best drill bits to use, the three most useful cutting burs, six different types of sanding bits, five ways to polish your work with the Foredom or Dremel, and five bits that can be used to add texture. In each category, I share my experience with the tool bits which save the most time, mention bench tips for getting the best results, and add cautions for safe use.

amazon.com/dp/0988285878/

Amazon Reader Review

- Five Stars - What a little treasure! … This book, while small, is packed full of great information on the subject. It's a great resource to keep handy at your bench.

Broom Casting For Creative Jewelry

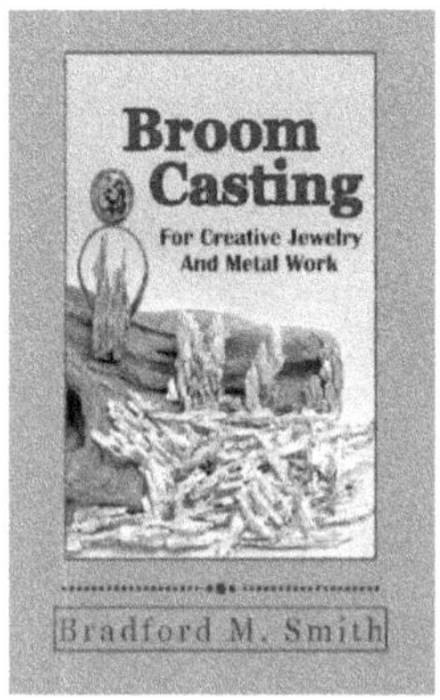

Discover the rush of pouring molten silver into a straw broom to get marvelous icicle-like shapes that just beg to be designed into finished jewelry like pendants and earrings.

Broom casting is a technique that yields beautiful results, doesn't require a lot of time to learn, and is just plain fun to do. In a couple hours you can be producing intriguing geometries that spark the imagination and challenge your creativity.

"Broom Casting For Creative Jewelry" gives step-by-step procedures for casting and covers proper use of all equipment. It includes how to work with the irregular shapes for your designs and has suggestions for safety, tips for cleaning& polishing, and ideas for making some of your own tools. Other sections cover how to run your own broom casting workshop for friends & club members and a gallery of finished jewelry utilizing some of the cast shapes.

amazon.com/dp/0988285835/

Amazon Reader Reviews

- I've found Broom Casting a little intimidated, but I love the look. So I was really excited to hear about this book. Brad Smith's book really takes the mystery out of the process. He breaks down the steps really well, and walks you through the process clearly and simply. Then he shows you how to look at, clean/cut, and finally create with the castings. He really covers this cool technique from top to bottom. It's all in this great little book.

- Broom Casting for Creative Jewelry outlines everything you need to know to start and continue broom casting silver.

Making Design Stamps for Jewelry

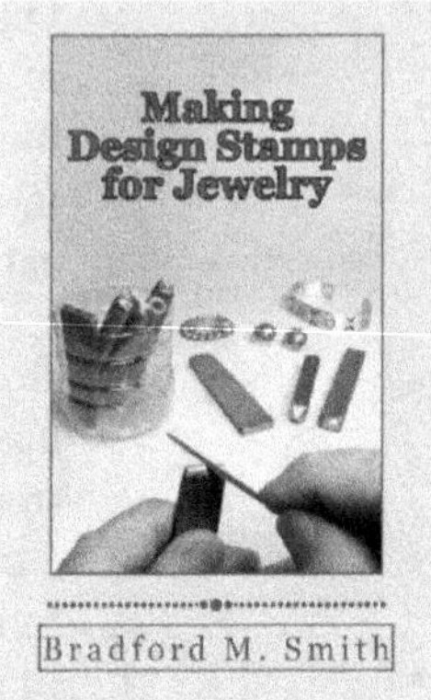

Learn how to create unique stamps and texturing tools to add visual interest to your work, for a special application, or to brand your pieces with a stamp that others cannot purchase. These customized tools embellish your jewelry designs and can be made with common jewelry tools and techniques. There are only a few differences in working with steel as compared to copper or silver.

The volume covers the step-by-step process of selecting best steels, carving the design, hardening the steel, and tempering it to ensure a long service life. It describes the tools to use, gives detailed examples for making several stamps, includes sources for tool steel, describes useful shop equipment, and has tips for saving time and achieving better quality.

amazon.com/dp/098828586X/

Editorial Review

"A must have book for the metalsmith"
- Danny Wade, Ferro Valley Tool, LLC and creator of the Metal Stamp Addicts group on Facebook.

Amazon Reader Review

- This book is absolutely wonderful! If you are at all interested in the very least in making your own jewelry stamps, then you definitely need this book. At 68 pages, I was initially hesitant, but I was wrong; this book is jam-packed with a plethora of information, all of which is totally relevant, and revealing

Broom Casting For Creative Jewelry

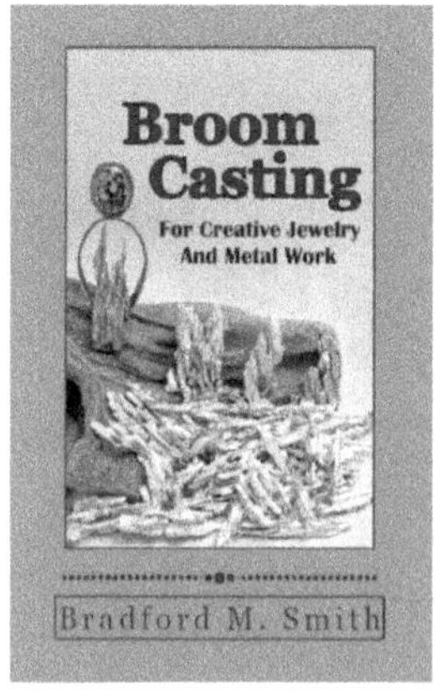

Discover the rush of pouring molten silver into a straw broom to get marvelous icicle-like shapes that just beg to be designed into finished jewelry like pendants and earrings.

Broom casting is a technique that yields beautiful results, doesn't require a lot of time to learn, and is just plain fun to do. In a couple hours you can be producing intriguing geometries that spark the imagination and challenge your creativity.

"Broom Casting For Creative Jewelry" gives step-by-step procedures for casting and covers proper use of all equipment. It includes how to work with the irregular shapes for your designs and has suggestions for safety, tips for cleaning& polishing, and ideas for making some of your own tools. Other sections include a gallery of finished jewelry utilizing some of the cast shapes.

amazon.com/dp/0988285835/

Amazon Reader Reviews

- I've found Broom Casting a little intimidated, but I love the look. So I was really excited to hear about this book. Brad Smith's book really takes the mystery out of the process. He breaks down the steps really well, and walks you through the process clearly and simply. Then he shows you how to look at, clean/cut, and finally create with the castings. He really covers this cool technique from top to bottom. It's all in this great little book.

- Broom Casting for Creative Jewelry and Metal Work outlines everything you need to know to start and continue broom casting silver.

The Reluctant Farmer of Whimsey Hill

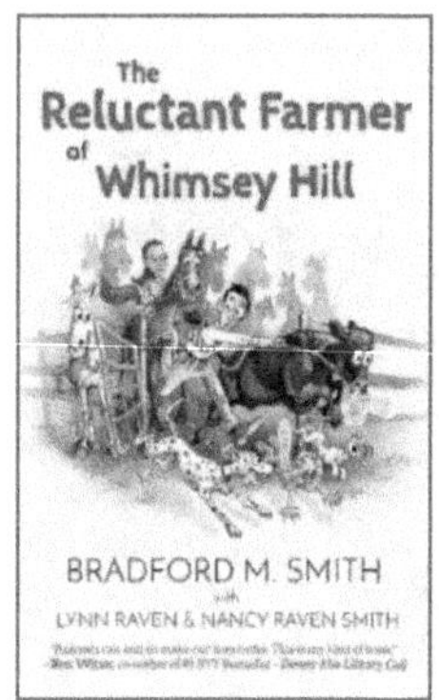

The Reluctant Farmer of Whimsey Hill is a light-hearted, true love story between more than a man and a woman. Imagine *Marley and Me*, not with one pesky dog, but with a farm full of quirky animals. The narrative follows Brad's fish-out-of-water point of view as a 25-year-old, animal-phobic, computer nerd from the city who moves to a rural, Virginia farm with his new, animal-loving bride. There he's propelled on a journey of self-discovery as his bride's crazy animals teach him about life and love - the hard way.

amazon.com/dp/0988285851/

Editorial Reviews

- Animals can and do make our lives better. This is my kind of book.

  - Bret Witter, #1 NYT bestseller co-author of Dewey [the Library Cat]

- A witty memoir reminding us that the best lessons in life are beyond the edge of one's comfort zone, and one can only be towed there by the heart strings."

  - Jean Abernethy, creator of Fergus the Horse

Amazon Reader Reviews

- Anyone who loves animals, has a sense of humor and appreciates a good, clean book (plenty of mud though) will love this book!

- A charming, witty, well written account of the country life of a young couple, with some sweet moments and some laugh out loud moments. We thoroughly enjoyed it.

INDEX

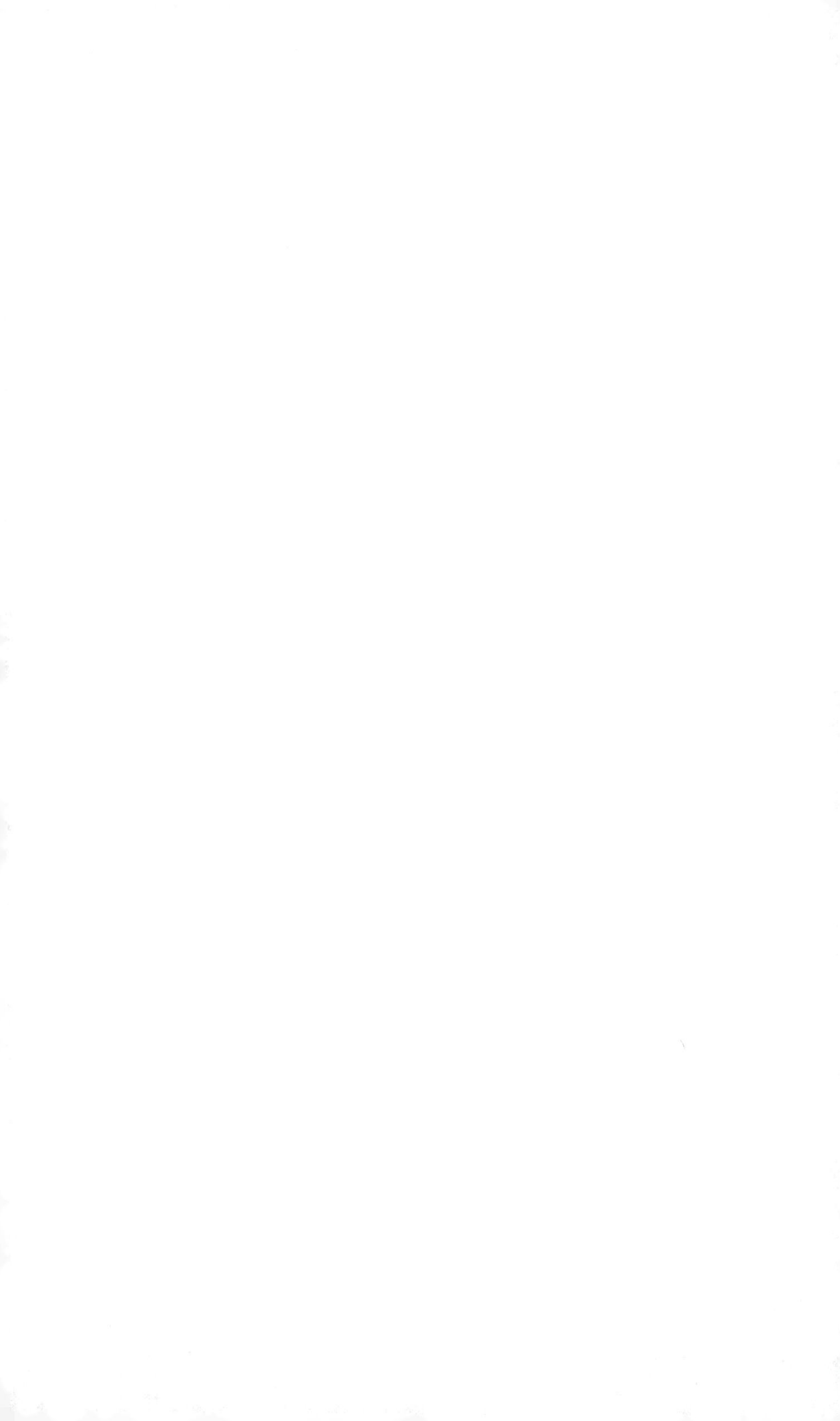

www.ingramcontent.com/pod-product-compliance
Lightning Source LLC
LaVergne TN
LVHW010938110826
845149LV00013B/2652

9780988285804